Current Chinese Economic Report Series

More information about this series at http://www.springer.com/series/11028

Center for Macroeconomic Research
of Xiamen University

China's Macroeconomic Outlook

Quarterly Forecast and Analysis Report, October 2017

By the China's Quarterly Macroeconometric Model (CQMM) team Center for Macroeconomic Research at Xiamen University

Springer

Center for Macroeconomic Research
of Xiamen University
Center for Macroeconomic Research
Xiamen University
Xiamen, Fujian
China

ISSN 2194-7937 ISSN 2194-7945 (electronic)
Current Chinese Economic Report Series
ISBN 978-981-10-8095-1 ISBN 978-981-10-8096-8 (eBook)
https://doi.org/10.1007/978-981-10-8096-8

Grants: the major projects of China National Social Science Foundation (15ZDC011, 13&ZD029), the major research projects of philosophy and social sciences of China's Ministry of Education of China (16JZD016, 15JZD016, 14JZD011), the key research projects of the Key Research Institutions of Humanities and Social Sciences at Universities (A Upgrade of CQMM), the project of China National Social Science Foundation (17BJY086, 15BJL008, 13CJL017), the youth project of China Natural Science Foundation (71503222).

Library of Congress Control Number: 2018930244

Printed on acid-free paper

This Springer imprint is published by the registered company Springer Nature Singapore Pte Ltd. part of Springer Nature
The registered company address is: 152 Beach Road, #21-01/04 Gateway East, Singapore 189721, Singapore

Preface

This report is a partial result of China's Quarterly Macroeconometric Model (CQMM), a project developed and maintained by the Center for Macroeconomic Research (CMR) of Xiamen University. The CMR is one of the Key Research Institutes of Humanities and Social Sciences sponsored by the Ministry of Education of China, focusing on China's economic forecast and macroeconomic policy analysis. The CMR started to develop the CQMM for the purpose of short-term forecasting, policy analysis, and simulation in 2005.

Based on the CQMM, the CMR and its partners hold press conferences to release forecasts for China' major macroeconomic variables. Since July, 2006, 22 quarterly reports on China's macroeconomic outlook have been presented and 11th annual reports have been published.

This 23rd quarterly report is to be presented at the Forum on China's Macroeconomic Outlook and Press Conference of CQMM on October 27, 2017. This conference is jointly held at Oxford University by Oxford Prospects and Global Development Centre, University of Oxford, Center for Macroeconomic Research at Xiamen University, and Economic Information Daily at Xinhua News Agency.

Xiamen, China

Center for Macroeconomic Research
of Xiamen University

Acknowledgements

According to the Chinese Pinyin order of their names, the 121 experts who joined this questionnaire survey were: Yongzu Bian, Peiwen Bo, Xin Chang, Changbing Chen, Gong Chen, Jianbao Chen, Jinmei Chen, Kunting Chen, Langnan Chen, Menggen Chen, Shoudong Chen, Yanbin Chen, Zhiyong Chen, Kuizao Dai, XiangDeng, Conglai Fan, Ziying Fan, Bo Gao, Qiyou Guo, Xibao Guo, Xiaohe Guo, Zhiyi Guo, Zhaozhou Han, Jingtong He, Maoxing Huang, Xianfeng Huang, Zhigang Huang, Erhcheng Hwa, Xinhua Jian, Yongmu Jiang, TaoJin, Chunqi Li, Haizheng Li, Jianwei Li, JunLi, Xuesong Li, Yingdong Li, Xuegui Lin, Fengliang Liu, Jianping Liu, Jinquan Liu, Qiongzhi Liu, Xiaoxin Liu, Yunzhong Liu, Zhibiao Liu, Ying Ma, Yue Ma, Shuijun Peng, Suling Peng, Wan-wen Chu, Ruoen Ren, Yihang Shao, Kunrong Shen, lisheng Shen, Junyi Shi, Jian Su, Wei Sun, Wei Tan, Jijun Tang, Ruzhu Tian, Changyun Wang, Hongju Wang, Tongsan Wang, Yida Wang, Cheng Wang, Dashu Wang, Guocheng Wang, Jiping Wang, Junbo Wang, Liyong Wang, Meijin Wang, Xi Wang, Yanxing Wang, Yongqin Wang, Yuesheng Wang, Chuanhao Wen, Xinru Wu, Xingzhi Xiao, Danyang Xie, Di Xie, Pan Xie, Xianxiang Xu, Yifan Xu, Bin Xu, Wenbin Xu, Ping Yan, Chengyu Yang, Cuihong Yang, Ruilong Yang, Chusheng Ye, XianrongYi, Xingmin Yin, Yi Heng, Li Yu, ZuoYu, Fuhua Yuan, XuhengZang, Jinli Zeng, Wuyi Zeng, Chengsi Zhang, Donghui Zhang, Liqun Zhang, Liancheng Zhang, Long Zhang, Mingzhi Zhang, Ping Zhang, Shuguang Zhang, Tao Zhang, Yishan Zhang, Changhui Zhao, Minghao Zhao, Xindong Zhao, Zhenquan Zhao, Zhijun Zhao, Chaoyu Zheng, Liqun Zhou, Zejiong Zhou, Baohua Zhu, Qigui Zhu, Jianping Zhu, Zongming Zhuang.

The experts who joined this questionnaire survey are from institutions including Baoshang Bank, Ministry of Finance, National Bureau of Statistics, Development Research Center of the State Council, Economic Information Daily, Ministry of Commerce, Tianze Institute of Economic Research, International Department, Central Committee of CPC, Academy of Mathematics and Systems Science, Chinese Academy of Sciences(CAS), Center for Forecasting Science of CAS, National Academy of Economic Strategy, Chinese Academy of Social Sciences

(CASS), Institute of Finance and Banking of CASS, Institute of Economics of CASS, Institute of Quantitative and Technical Economics of CASS, China Banking Association, The Export-Import Bank of China, Chung-Hua Institution for Economic Research, Taiwan Academia Sinica and universities including Anhui University of Finance and Economics, Peking University, BeiHang University, Beijing Normal University, Chongqing Technology and Business University, Dongbei University of Finance and Economics, Fujian Normal University, Fudan University, Fuzhou University, Guangxi University, East China Normal University, Huaqiao University, Hunan University, Jilin University, Jinan University, Liaoning University, Lanzhou University, Nanjing University, Nankai University, Shandong University, Shaanxi Normal University, Shanghai University of Finance and Economics, Shanghai University of International Business and Economics, Shanghai Jiao Tong University, Capital University of Economics and Business, Sichuan University, National Taiwan University, Tianjin University of Finance and Economics, Tianjin University of Commerce, Wuhan University, Xi'an Jiaotong University, Northwest University, Xiamen University, National University of Singapore, Hong Kong University of Science and Technology, City University of Hong Kong, Zhejiang University of Finance & Economics, Zhejiang University of Technology, Renmin University of China, Zhongnan University of Economics and Law, China Europe International Business School, Sun Yat-sen University, Central University of Finance and Economics, etc.

For the active participation and insights of all above-mentioned experts, we wish to extend our deep thanks.

Principal Investigator

Min Gong

Research Team Members

Wenpu Li, Zhiyuan Lin, Yu Liu, Shengrong Lu, Guifu Chen, Changlin Yu, Yanwu Wang, Jing Li, Huakun Wu

The Chinese edition of this report is contributed by Changlin Yu, Huakun Wu, Yanwu Wang, Zhiyuan Lin, and Guifu Chen. It is revised by Wenpu Li and Min Gong, and translated by Zhiyuan Lin and Guifu Chen. The raw data are processed by Huakun Wu.

Contents

Executive Summary

In the first half of 2017, China's economy went stronger than expected. The real GDP grew by 6.9% in the first and second quarter, respectively. From the perspective of the demand side, such rapid growth was driven by rebounded exports arising from the global economic recovery, strong growth in real estate investment, rapid expansion in infrastructure construction investment, and resilience of consumption growth.

From the second half of 2017 through the end of 2018, the global economic recovery is expected to continue boosting China's foreign trade growth. In addition, the ongoing supply-side structural reforms and the steady growth of domestic consumer demand are anticipated to continue to tamp the foundation of China's economic growth. Nevertheless, such factors as high corporate and local debt ratios strengthened supervision on the systemic financial risks, and measures to harness the property market are anticipated to continue curbing the rapid growth of investment.

According to the China Quarterly Macroeconometric Model (CQMM) under some key assumptions on exogenous variable, China's economic growth is projected to edge up, and the inflation rate is expected to remain at a moderate and stable level.

1. Real GDP growth is expected to increase by 6.8% in 2017, 0.1 percentage points higher than that in 2016. The CPI is set to expand by 1.72%, 0.29 percentage points higher over 2016. The PPI is forecast to rise by 6.24%, up by 7.59 percentage points over 2016. The GDP deflator is anticipated to pick up by 4.77%, 3.65 percentage points higher than that of 2016.
2. The industrial production is expected to grow steadily, private investment is projected to rebound, and the fixed-asset investment (excluding farmers) is forecast to edge down. In 2017, the fixed-asset investment in current prices term is anticipated to grow by 8.55% in 2017, up by 0.21 percentage points over 2016.

3. The growth of real disposable income of urban and rural residents is expected to diverse, the growth of urban residents' income is speeding up, while the growth of rural residents' income is slowing down. Measured at current prices, the total retail sales of consumer goods in 2017 are expected to grow by 10.69%, up by 0.23 percentage points over 2016.
4. Strong performance of the global economy is expected to continue boosting China's exports over the projection horizon. Measured at current prices, the value of exports in U.S. dollars is expected to grow by 7.9% in 2017, up by 14.37 percentage points over 2016. The value of imports is projected to rise by 16.18%, markedly up by 21.79 percentage points over 2016.

Coping with systemic financial risks is currently on the high agenda of China's policy making. Our CQMM team observes that the high leverage of the nonfinancial SOEs is the main cause of financial risks. Based on this observation, the policy simulation of this report aims to explore the macroeconomic effects of putting hard budget constraint on the SOEs. The main idea of the policy simulation is: in order to control systemic financial risks from the source, we need to tighten the money supply first. Under the quantitative deleveraging policy of tightening money supply gradually, the model sets two different scenarios: one is that the SOEs face soft budget constraint, the other is that the SOEs face hard budget constraint.

The policy simulation results show that in the case that the SOEs face soft budget constraint, it cannot effectively reduce financial risks simply by reducing M2 growth and withdrawing money. First, under China's current government-led economic system, governments at all levels have strong motives to boost economic growth. As there exists close relationship between the SOEs and governments, to achieve the goal of policy, governments at all levels would strive to help the SOEs obtain credit line, which make the leverage of the SOEs hard to decrease. Even if the M2 growth is reduced by 3 percentage points, the leverage of the SOEs at the end of the simulation period is higher than the actual reference value by 0.25 percentage points.

Second, the fact that the SOEs face the soft budget constraint is in essence give them priority to obtain credit resources in the cast of tight funds, which would shift most of the credit crunch pressure to non-SOEs. Such mechanism would not only have great impact on the growth of private investment growth but also lead to the decline of overall social investment efficiency. As a result, economic growth would be dragged down significantly, and the motive of the local government to boost economic growth by increasing leverage would be strengthened further.

Based on the above observations and policy simulation results, the CQMM team suggests the following policies to counter the systemic financial risks in China's economy:

1. The local government should shift its focus on stimulating local economic growth to provide more public goods and services.
2. Establish a standard and rigorous modern government budget system as soon as possible, and put hard budget constraints on the local governments and the SOEs.
3. Take measures to withdraw excessively issued money gradually.
4. Fully make use of various financial means to reduce the leverage of the non-SOEs.
5. Strengthen the supervision on the shadow banking and make the financial system return to its intrinsic functions of allocating economic resources.

Chapter 1
China's Economic Performance in the First Half of 2017

1.1 Overview

In the first half of 2017, the Chinese economy went stronger than expected. The real GDP grew by 6.9% in the first and second quarter, respectively. The overall employment was in good condition. An additional 7.35 million urban jobs were created, 0.18 million jobs more than that in the same period last year.

From the perspective of the supply side, the rebound of industrial production, especially manufacturing, is the main reason. Industrial production registered a stable performance with good momentum for growth. In the first half of 2017, the value added of industrial enterprises above the designed size went up by 6.9%.

From the perspective of the demand side, China's rapid economic growth in the first half of 2017 was driven by factors such as rebounded exports due to the global economic recovery, strong growth in real estate investment, rapid expansion in infrastructure construction investment, and resilience of consumption growth.

Consumer goods prices and industrial product prices maintained stable in the first half of 2017. As food prices stayed low, the monthly consumer price index (CPI) growth rates fluctuated between 0.8 and 2.5%. Affected by the international commodity prices fluctuations and the domestic supply-side reform, the monthly producer price index (PPI) growth all exceeded 5.5%. Due to moderate inflation rates, China's monetary policy maintained slightly tight in the context of strengthening financial supervision. The broad money (M2) growth rates declined from 11.3% in January to 9.4% in June.

Thanks to the resilience of China's economy and the rapid development of real estate, in the first half of 2017, revenues in China's general public budget picked up by 10.3%, while proceeds from transferring state-owned land-use rights surged by 34%. Owing to rapid expansion of the people's livelihood expenditure items, expenditures in China's general public budget continued to grow strongly. In the first half of 2017, the fiscal deficit amounted to $917.7 billion, a substantial increase of $552.6 billion over the same period of a year earlier.

China's Macroeconomic Outlook, Current Chinese Economic Report Series,
https://doi.org/10.1007/978-981-10-8096-8_1

Generally speaking, in the first half of 2017, the Chinese economy showed the following characteristics: (1) China's GDP growth and the growth of industrial value added both exceeded projections, and equipment industries continued expanding strongly. (2) Improved exports and inventory replenishment boosted the growth of industrial value added. (3) Both private investment and manufacturing investment improved, and infrastructure investment swelled rapidly. (4) Housing sales went strong, and the third and fourth-tier cities reduced real state inventory rapidly. (5) Employment, residential income, and consumption picked up, and rural consumption pulled up the overall consumption. (6) Prices remained stable, and supply-side contraction pushed up industrial prices. (7) The growth of M2 continued to slow down, and strengthened financial supervision did not hinder social funds from supporting the real economy. (8) Proceeds from transferring state-owned land-use rights increased substantially, while the fiscal deficit expanded strongly.

1.2 Both GDP Growth and the Growth of Industrial Value Added Exceeded Projections, and Equipment Industries Continued to Expand Strongly

In the first half of 2017, China's real GDP grew by 6.9%, up by 0.2 percentage points (pcs) over the same period last year, exceeding market expectations (see Fig. 1.1).

Fig. 1.1 GDP growth exceeded projections. *Source* CQMM team calculations on CEIC data

In the first quarter of 2017, China's real GDP rose by 6.9%, up 0.1 pcs compared with that in the previous quarter. By sector, industrial value added went up 0.4 pcs, boosting GDP growth by 0.13 pcs. Growth in agriculture, wholesale and retail trades, financial intermediation, and real estate, all rebounded. Dragging factors mainly included construction; transportation, storage, and postal services; especially 'other services', of which growth rate fell by 1.4 pcs, pulling down GDP growth by 0.28 pcs, and the reason is not clear (see Table 1.1).

In the second quarter, China's real GDP increased by 6.9%, unchanged from that in the previous quarter. By sector, industrial value added picked up slightly, which provided main support for the stable GDP growth. Value added in agriculture, construction, transportation, storage, and postal services rebounded. Dragging-down factors mainly came from financial intermediation, real estate, and other services. Due to strengthened financial supervision and the impact of shrunk stock market transaction, value added growth of financial intermediation declined. Due to the slowdown in commercial housing sales, value added growth of real estate went down (see Table 1.1).

In the first half of 2017, the value added of industrial enterprises above the designed size increased by 6.9%, up 0.9 pcs over the same period a year earlier. In June, the value added of industrial enterprises above the designed size went up by 7.6%, a significant increase of 1.1 pcs compared with that in May 2017. Both exceeded market expectations (see Fig. 1.2).

By sector, in the case of equipment industries, except that value added of railways, ships, aerospace and other transport equipment manufacturing hovered in low growth, value added of others sectors, such as general-purpose equipment industry, special-purpose equipment industry, electrical machinery and equipment industry, computer, communications and other electronic equipment industry, continued to expand rapidly, with its growth rate exceeding 12% in June 2017, almost doubling that of industrial value added (see Fig. 1.3).

1.3 Improved Exports and Inventory Replenishment Boosted the Growth of Industrial Value Added

Improved foreign trade provided important support for the rebound of China's GDP growth. In the first and second quarter of 2017, the contribution of net exports of goods and services to GDP was 4.2 and 3.9%, respectively, up 15.7 pcs and 14.3 pcs over the same period a year earlier (see Fig. 1.4).

That exports went strong was an important driver of the rise in the growth of industrial value added. In the first and second quarter of 2017, measured by current US dollar, value of exports grew by 4.2 and 6.3% respectively, up 13.9 pcs and 10.7 pcs over the same period last year. Growth of volume of exports also changed markedly, from declining 12.5% in the second quarter of 2016, narrowing down to

Table 1.1 Real GDP growth by sector

	GDP	Primary industry	Secondary industry	Tertiary industry	Industry	Construction	Wholesale and retail trades	Transportation, storage, and postal services	Accommodation and catering services	Financial intermediation	Real estate	Other services
% YoY changes, 2016Q4	6.80	2.90	6.10	8.30	6.10	5.90	7.20	9.90	7.30	3.80	7.70	10.60
% YoY changes, 2017Q1	6.90	3.00	6.40	7.70	6.50	5.30	7.40	8.70	7.40	4.40	7.80	9.20
Pcs YoY changes	0.10	0.10	0.30	−0.60	0.40	−0.60	0.20	−1.20	0.10	0.60	0.10	−1.40
Effects on GDP growth, pcs YoY changes		0.01	0.12	−0.31	0.13	−0.04	0.02	−0.05	0.00	0.05	0.01	−0.28
% YoY changes, 2017Q1	6.90	3.00	6.40	7.70	6.50	5.30	7.40	8.70	7.40	4.40	7.80	9.20
% YoY changes, 2017Q2	6.90	3.80	6.40	7.60	6.60	5.40	7.10	9.60	7.00	3.20	6.20	7.20
Pcs YoY changes	0.00	0.80	0.00	−0.10	0.10	0.10	−0.30	0.90	−0.40	−1.20	−1.60	−2.00
Effects on GDP growth, pcs YoY changes		0.05	0.00	−0.05	0.03	0.01	−0.03	0.04	−0.01	−0.11	−0.11	−0.44

Note (a) 'pcs' denotes percentage points. (b) 'Effects on GDP growth' = growth rates of sectoral product * the proportion of sectoral product in GDP in the same quarter of the previous year. (c) The total effects on GDP growth, which sum up each sub-item, are not equal to overall changes in GDP growth rates, because the table does not list all sectors.
Source CQMM team calculations on CEIC data

Fig. 1.2 The growth of industrial value added exceeded projections. *Source* CQMM team calculations on CEIC data

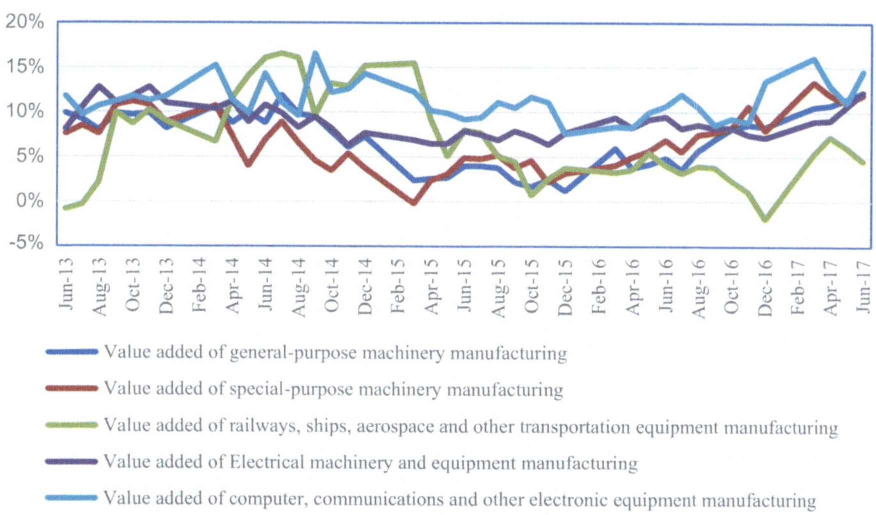

Fig. 1.3 Value added of equipment industries grew rapidly. *Source* CQMM team calculations on CEIC data

3.8% in the first quarter of 2017, and turning to rise 16.9% in the second quarter of 2017 (see Fig. 1.5).

The Figure of the delivery value of industrial product exports can also verify for this purpose. In the first half of 2017, the monthly growth of the delivery value of exports rebounded to over 10%, with 12.6 and 11.7% in March and June,

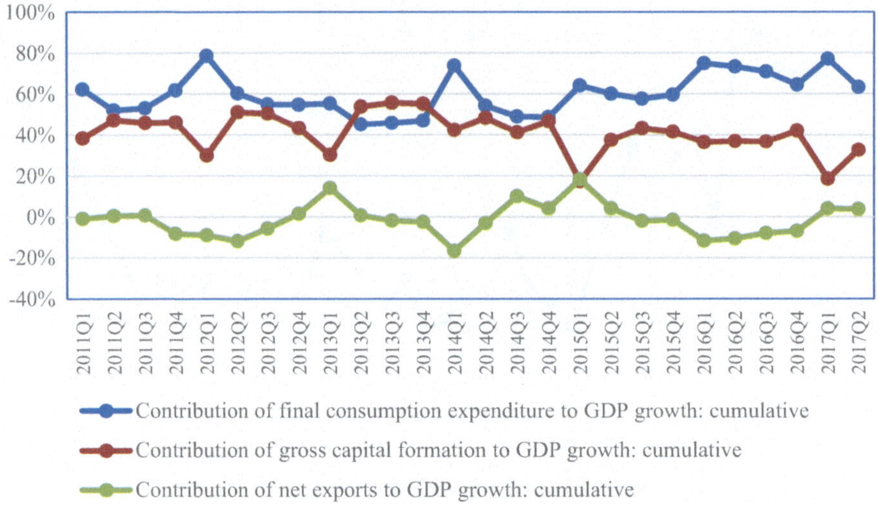

Fig. 1.4 Contribution of net exports to GDP growth turned from negative to positive. *Source* CQMM team calculations on CEIC data

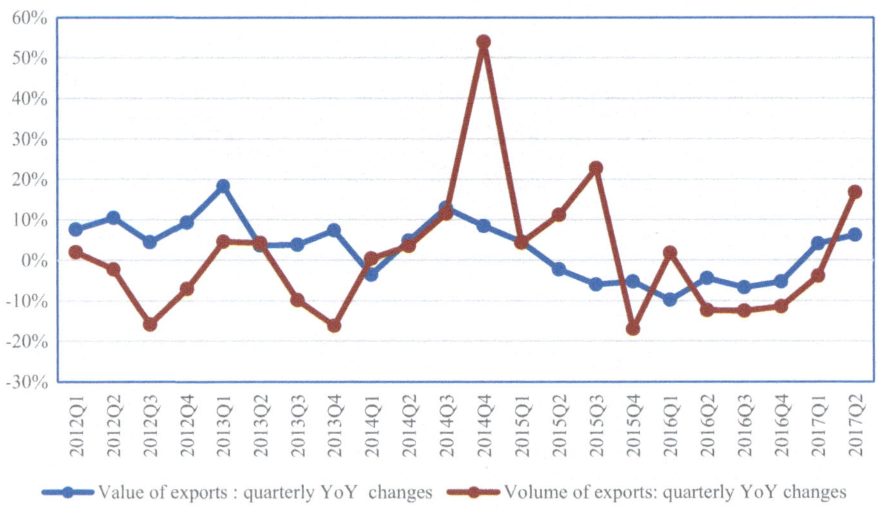

Fig. 1.5 Both value and volume of exports swelled. *Source* CQMM team calculations on CEIC data

respectively, which was the highest and the second highest since 2013 (see Fig. 1.6). The recovery of export industry chain was an important driving force to support the high growth of industrial value added.

In addition, inventory replenishment also provided support for production activities. In the first half of 2017, the growth of value added of three industries,

Fig. 1.6 Export delivery value rose markedly. *Source* CQMM team calculations on CEIC data

namely, raw chemical materials and chemical products manufacturing, smelting and pressing of ferrous metals, and smelting and pressing of non-ferrous metals, went up markedly (see Fig. 1.7). Although they were still in low levels, signs of raw material inventory replenishment could be seen obviously.

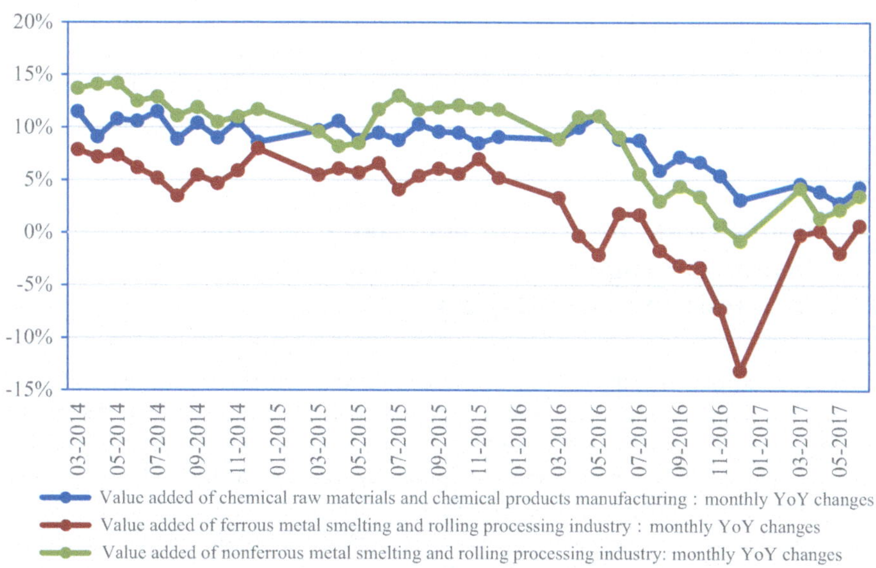

Fig. 1.7 Value added of raw material restocking industries picked up. *Source* CQMM team calculations on CEIC data

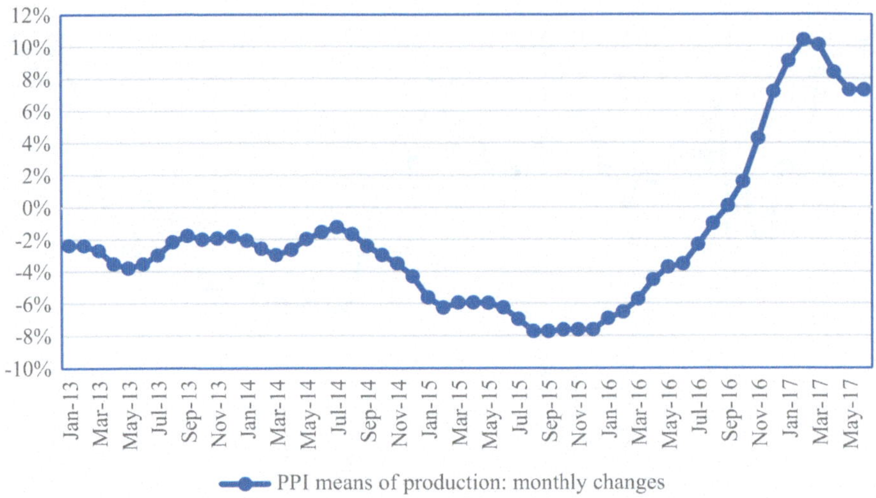

Fig. 1.8 The price index of means of production stayed high growth. *Source* CQMM team calculations on CEIC data

Inventory replenishment was also reflected by the changes in prices of means of production. In January 2017, the price index of means of production rose by 10.4%, reaching the peak since the outbreak of the global financial crisis in September 2008. Though its growth has slowed down since then, the month-on-month decline narrowed gradually, and in June 2017 remained as high as 7.3%. The high price index of means of production was closely related to the inventory replenishment (see Fig. 1.8). There are two factors contributing to inventory replenishment: one is the reversal of previous economic gloomy expectations, the other is incentives arising from exports improvement.

1.4 Both Private Investment and Manufacturing Investment Improved, and Infrastructure Investment Swelled Rapidly

In the first half of 2017, the total investment in fixed assets (FAI) grew by 8.6%, 0.4 pcs less than that in the same period last year, but 0.9 pcs more than that in the previous year. The private FAI rose by 7.2%, up 4.4 pcs over the same period last year, an increase of 4 pcs over the previous year (see Fig. 1.9).

The bland performance of the total FAI confirmed the above-mentioned viewpoint that improved exports and inventory replenishment boosted economic growth and industrial value added. Meanwhile, the improvement of private investment may

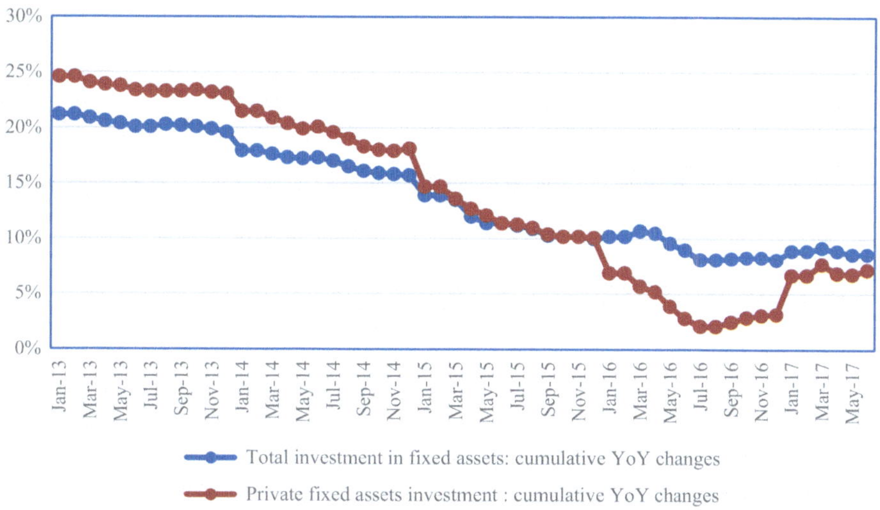

Fig. 1.9 The total FAI grew steadily and the private investment improved. *Source* CQMM team calculations on CEIC data

be attribute to the rebound of real economy, the promotion of public-and-private partnership (PPP) projects, and the mixed ownership reform.

In terms of the three major categories of investment, in the first half of 2017, the cumulative FAI in manufacturing grew by 5.5%, up 2.2 pcs over the same period last year, an increase of 1.4 pcs over the previous year. Investment in infrastructure construction increased by 21.1%, up 0.2 pcs compared with that in the same period last year, an increase of 3.7 pcs over the previous year. Investment in real estate rose by 5.5%, down 1.7% over the same period last year, down 1.3% over the previous year (see Fig. 1.10).

1.5 Housing Sales Went Strong, and the Third and Fourth-Tier Cities Reduced Real Estate Inventory Rapidly

In the first half of 2017, the total sales area and sales of commercial housing increased by 16.1 and 21.5% respectively, staying at relatively high levels. The new construction area of houses grew by 10.6%. That the growth of sales was greater than that of the new construction indicates that the speed of reducing real estate inventory was accelerating.

In the first half of 2017, the acceleration of reducing real estate inventory were mainly concentrated in the third and fourth-ties cities. Since the fourth quarter of 2016, in the first and second-tier cities, the growth of sales area of commercial

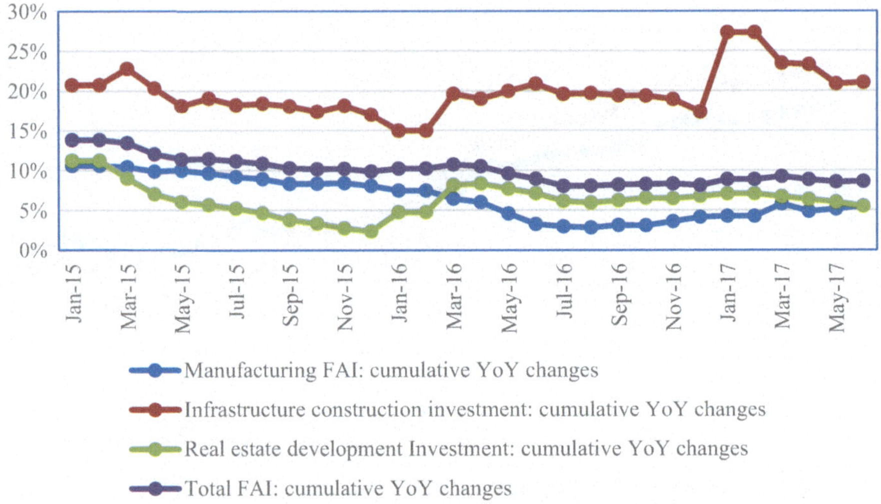

Fig. 1.10 Investment in manufacturing and infrastructure construction rebounded, while the growth of real estate investment slowed down. *Source* CQMM team calculations on CEIC data. *Note* Due to the lack of data, the Figure of investment in infrastructure construction in January 2015 to March 2015, and May 2016, was replaced by the sum of FAI in three industries, namely, electricity, heat, gas, and water production and supply, transportation, storage, and postal services; water conservancy, environment, and public facilities management, as the cumulative growth rates of them in the rest of months are almost the same

housing, sales of commercial housing, and the new construction area of housing have all shown significant declines. In May 2017 and June 2017, the growth of sales area of commercial housing in the first-tier cities even dropped by more than 25%. In contrast, in the third and fourth-tier cities, the growth of commercial housing sales and new housing construction maintained strong, and the growth of sales is higher than that of the new housing construction, showing that new measures taken since the four quarter of 2016 to regulate the property market in the first and second-tier cities had reversed the markets expectation at least in the short term (see Figs. 1.11, 1.12, and 1.13). Ample liquidity had flowed into the third and fourth-tier cities, stimulating the property market in the third or fourth-tier cities to pick up.

It is noteworthy that the quick reduction of real estate inventory in the third-tier and fourth-tier cities was not entirely the result of loose liquidity and changes in expectation of house prices. The accelerating implement of the monetized resettlement plan, under which people affected by rebuilding in rundown urban areas can receive monetary compensation, also played an important role. In 2016, the sold residential housing area involved in this plan reached 250 million square meters, accounting for 18.2% of the residential commercial housing sales area. In 2017, it is expected to reach 310 million square meters, and its proportion in the property market is set to swell further.

Fig. 1.11 Commercial housing sales area in third-tier cities expanded markedly. *Source* CQMM team calculations on CEIC data. *Note* The data shown in Figs. 1.10, 1.11, and 1.12 are related to 40 large and medium-sized cities, of which includes 4 first-tier cities: Beijing, Shanghai, Guangzhou, Shenzhen, 23 second-tier cities: Tianjin, Chongqing, Hangzhou, Nanjing, Wuhan, Shenyang, Chengdu, Xi'An, Dalian, Qingdao, Ningbo, Suzhou, Changsha, Jinan, Xiamen, Changchun, Harbin, Taiyuan, Zhengzhou, Hefei, Nanchang, Fuzhou, Shijiazhuang; and 13 three-tier cities: Wuxi, Guiyang, Kunming, Nanning, Beihai, Haikou, Sanya, Hohhot, Lanzhou, Wenzhou, Xining, Yinchuan, Urumqi

Fig. 1.12 Commercial housing sales in third-tier cities rose significantly. *Source* CQMM team calculations on CEIC data

Fig. 1.13 New housing construction area in third-tier cities picked up rapidly, but its growth was slower than that of housing sales area. *Source* CQMM team calculations on CEIC data

1.6 Employment, Residential Income, and Consumption Picked up, and Rural Consumption Pushed up the Overall Consumption

In the first half of 2017, a total of 7.35 million new urban jobs was created, an increase of 0.18 million over the same period last year. The real per capita disposable income rose by 7.3%, up 0.8% than that in the same period a year earlier. Migrant workers' wages rose 6.3% year-on-year, slightly down 0.2% compared with that in the same period last year (see Fig. 1.14).

The improvement in employment, residential income, and wages led to a steady increase in consumption growth. In the first half of 2017, the monthly average growth rate of retail sales of consumer goods was 10.4%, almost unchanged from that in the second half of 2016. The growth rate in June stood at 11% for the first time after 2016 (see Fig. 1.15).

Compared with the relatively stable urban consumption growth, rural consumption growth kept climbing after the four quarter of 2016. In June 2017, the total retail sales of consumer goods in rural areas rose by 12.9%, hitting a new high in 32 months, while in the second quarter grew by 12.7%. The rapid growth of rural consumption played a significant role in boosting the overall consumption (see Fig. 1.16).

There are two main causes for the accelerating growth of rural consumption: first, with the reduction in the ability of the first and second-tier cities to absorb migrant workers, some farmers chose to work in the third or fourth-tier cities near their hometowns, and second, some industries and shopping malls sank to the third

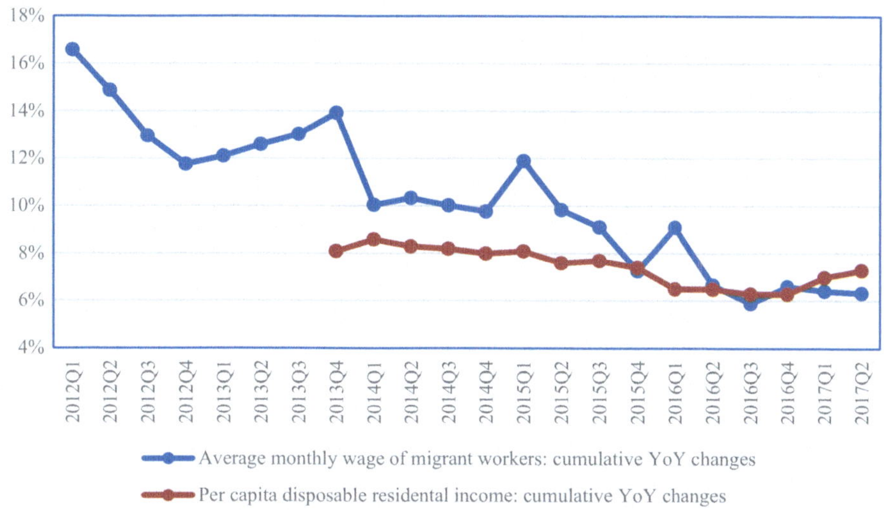

Fig. 1.14 Residents 'income continued to pick up and migrant workers' wages slightly slowed down. *Source* CQMM team calculations on CEIC data

Fig. 1.15 The growth of total retail sales of consumer goods was on the rise. *Source* CQMM team calculations on CEIC data

or fourth-tier cities, where can create more jobs for farmers. When the average annual income of farmers reached between 3000 and 5000 dollars, consumption escalation occurred, resulting in a rapid growth of consumption both in the third or fourth-tier cities and the rural areas.

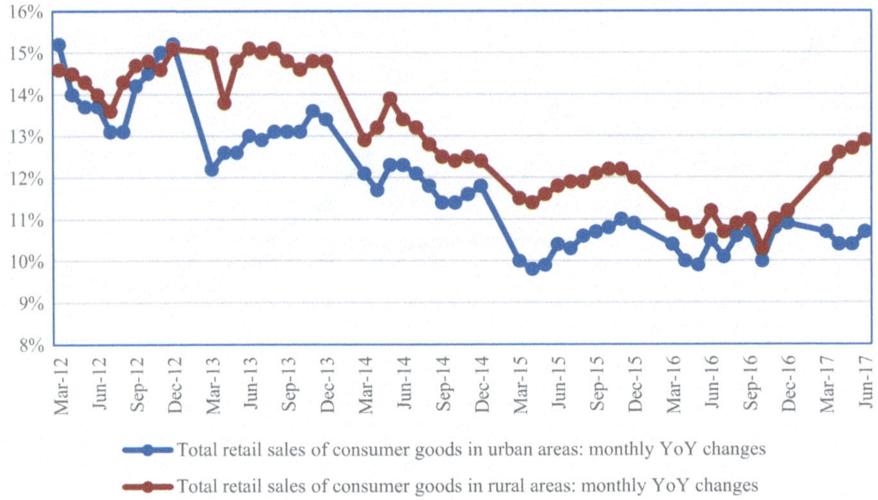

Fig. 1.16 Rural consumption grew faster than urban consumption. *Source* CQMM team calculations on CEIC data

1.7 Prices Remained Stable, and Supply-Side Contraction Pushed up Industrial Prices

In the first half of 2017, the prices of consumer goods and industrial products stayed stable. The CPI grew by 2.5% in January as a result of rising food prices during the Spring Festival, while in the rest of the months fluctuating between 0.8 and 1.5%. The producer price index (PPI), which is mainly affected by international prices fluctuations and China's domestic supply-side reform, rose above 5.5% monthly (see Fig. 1.17).

In the first half of 2017, the prices of industrial products generally maintained high growth, though their growth began to slow after February. As mentioned earlier, the rise in the growth of industrial prices was first due to increased international demand, followed by the contraction of the supply side. Specifically, the inspection on the substandard steel products, which was carried out in the first half of 2017, resulted in supply contraction and pushed up the industrial prices, which further boosted the demand for inventory replenishment, making the inventory of steel and other raw materials rebound to a certain degree, and thus formed positive feedback effect on the prices of industrial products (see Fig. 1.18).

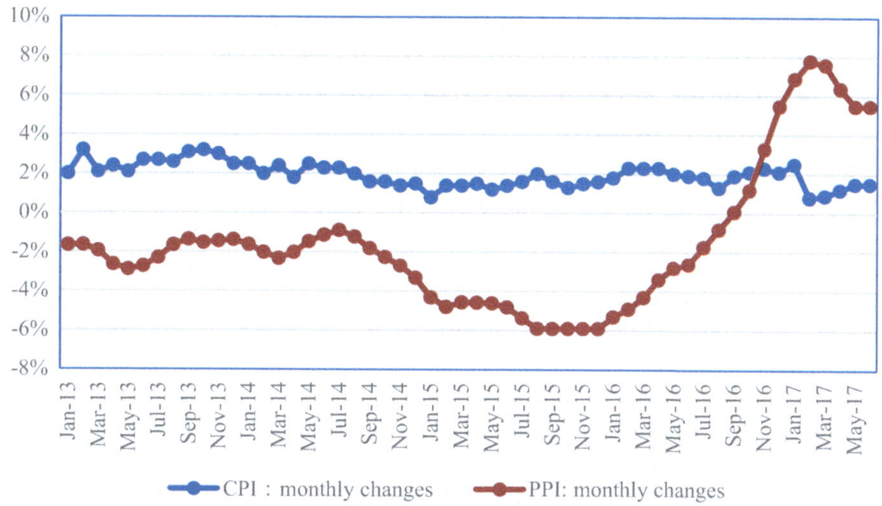

Fig. 1.17 The CPI remained stable, and the PPI stayed high. *Source* CQMM team calculations on CEIC data

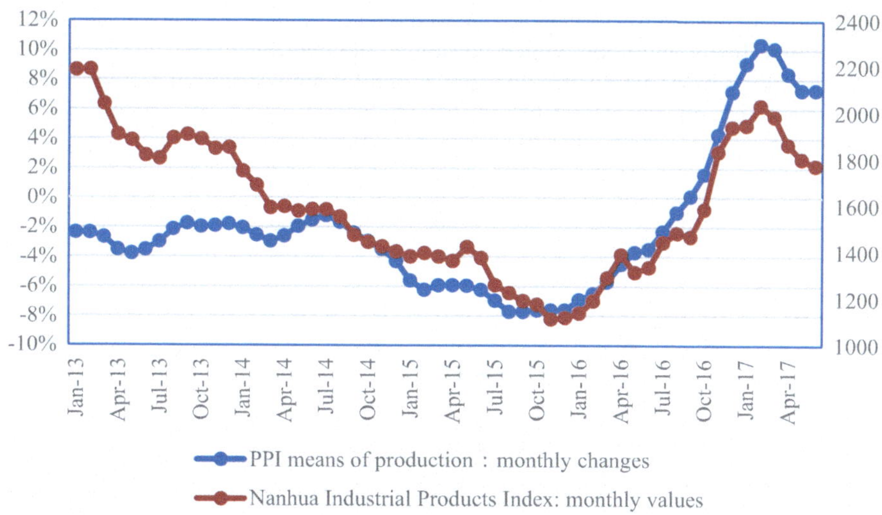

Fig. 1.18 The prices of industrial products maintained high growth. *Source* CQMM team calculations on Wind Info. *Note* The Nanhua Industrial Index has been processed into monthly averages

1.8 The Growth of M2 Continued to Slow Down, and Strengthened Financial Supervision Did not Hinder Social Funds from Supporting the Real Economy

In the first half of 2017, due to moderate price growth, China's monetary policy kept marginally tight. The M2 grew from 11.3% in January to 9.4% in June, down 2.7 and 2.4 pcs over the same period last year, respectively. In addition, its growth rate in June hit a record low. In contrast, social financing maintained a steady growth, which increased by 12.8%, slightly up 0.4 pcs over the same period a year earlier (see Fig. 1.19).

As M2 is mainly made up of deposit, let us take a look at the change in deposits. The total amount of deposits was down by 1.79 pcs from December 2016 to June 2017. Of which, the effect of the decline in the growth of corporate deposits was as high as 1.92 pcs, while the changes in the growth of other three items, namely, fiscal deposits, savings deposits, and non-banking financial institutions deposits, only had weak effects on the growth of overall deposits (see Table 1.2).

And thus, the slowdown in the growth of corporate deposits was the main cause for the sustained decline in M2 growth in the first half of 2017. And the slowdown in corporate deposits growth may be due to the increase in real economic activities, such as investment and trade, which consumed the deposit funds.

In the past several years, the financial turmoil mainly occurred in the shadow banking system and the internet financial fields. In order to avoid systemic risks in finance and economy, the rapid expansion of shadow banking and the brutal growth

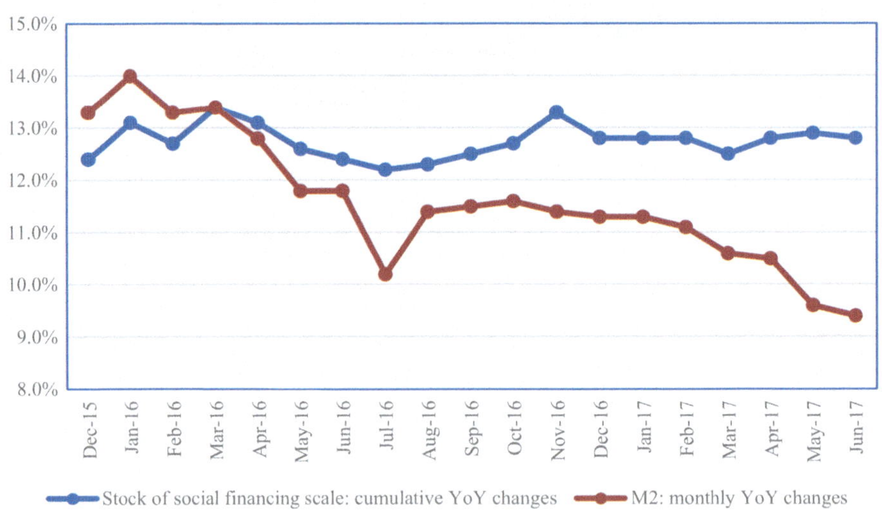

Fig. 1.19 The growth of M2 and that of social financing scale diverged. *Source* CQMM team calculations on CEIC data

Table 1.2 Growth of deposits by sector

	Total deposit	Corporate deposit	Government deposit	Savings deposit	Non-banking financial institutions deposit
2016/12, %	10.97	16.72	2.44	9.46	7.05
2017/6, %	9.18	9.56	8.66	9.56	8.66
% YoY changes, pcs	−1.79	−5.84	−12.03	0.10	1.62
Effects on total deposit, pcs YoY changes		−1.92	−0.29	0.04	0.40

Note (1) pcs mean percentage points. (2) 'Effects on total deposit, % YoY changes' = sectoral % YoY changes * the proportion of sectoral deposit in total deposit. *Source* CQMM team calculations on CEIC data

of internet finance must be curbed. Since the end of March 2017, China's regulators have strengthened the regulation and governance of shadow banking and internet finance. Many initiatives have been implemented.

The strong signal that regulators released in the first half 2017 to strengthen financial regulations had obviously affected the market liquidity. What effects did the strengthened financial supervision have on the Chinese economy?

As we know, the broad money M2 represents the social funds input by the central bank via the commercial banks, while the social financing structure denotes the various channels by which various social sectors obtain funds. The strengthened financial supervision has changed the social financing structure. In the first quarter of 2017, off-balance-sheet loans, which mainly made up of entrusted loans, trust loan, and bank's acceptance bill not discounted, accounted for 29.52% of the social financing. Affected by the strengthened financial supervision started at end of March 2017, off-balance-sheet loans accounted for only 10.18% of social financing, a decrease of 19.34 pcs, indicating a significant contraction (see Fig. 1.20).

In terms of off-balance-sheet financing, part of loan demand had to get out from the original channels, namely, entrusted loan and bank's acceptance bill not discount, to trust loan, a normal off-balance-sheet channel which is counted in the social financing, and thus became a part of new incremental social financing. With this shift, it provided a certain supporting role for the steady growth of social financing (see Fig. 1.21).

Consistent with the downward trend in the growth of M2, in the first half of 2017, the growth of domestic credit also continued to decline. As to the credit structure, it can be found that the growth of creditor's rights of deposit companies on non-bank financial institutions and the government sector showed an obvious declining trend, while the growth of creditor's rights on non-financial businesses remained fairly stable (see Figs. 1.22 and 1.23).

Therefore, the main causes for the decline in credit growth are: on the one hand, commercial banks tightened lending to non-bank financial institutions, such as

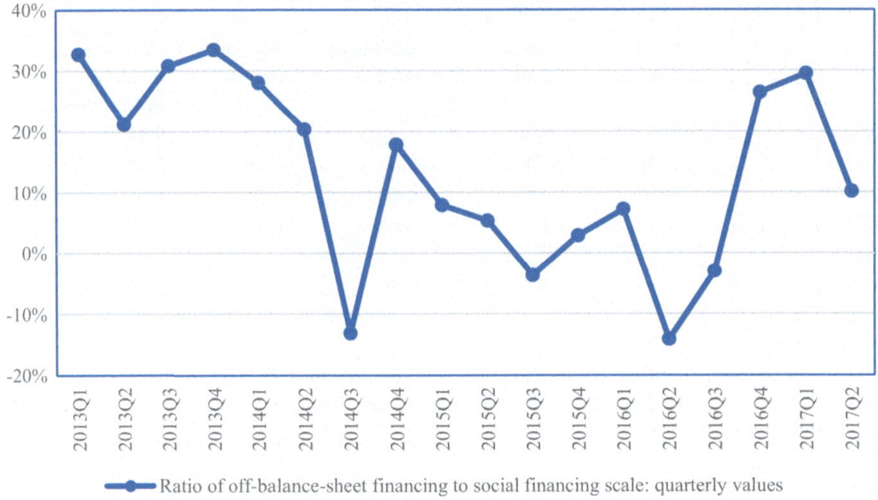

Fig. 1.20 Off-balance-sheet financing shrank markedly. *Note* Off-balance-sheet financing = entrusted loan + trust loan + bank's acceptance bill not discounted. *Source* CQMM team calculations on CEIC data

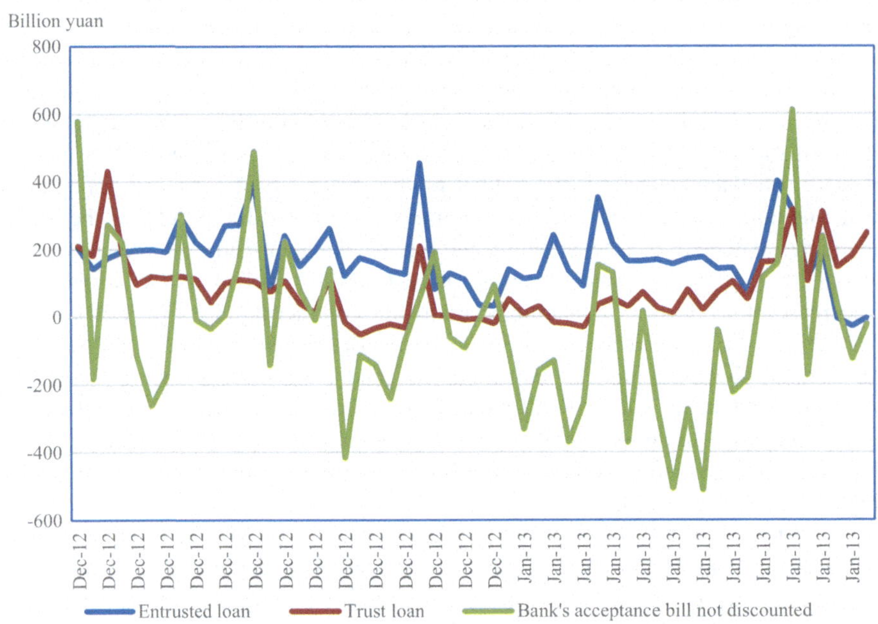

Fig. 1.21 Off-balance-sheet financing increment mainly came from trust loans. *Source* CQMM team calculations on CEIC data

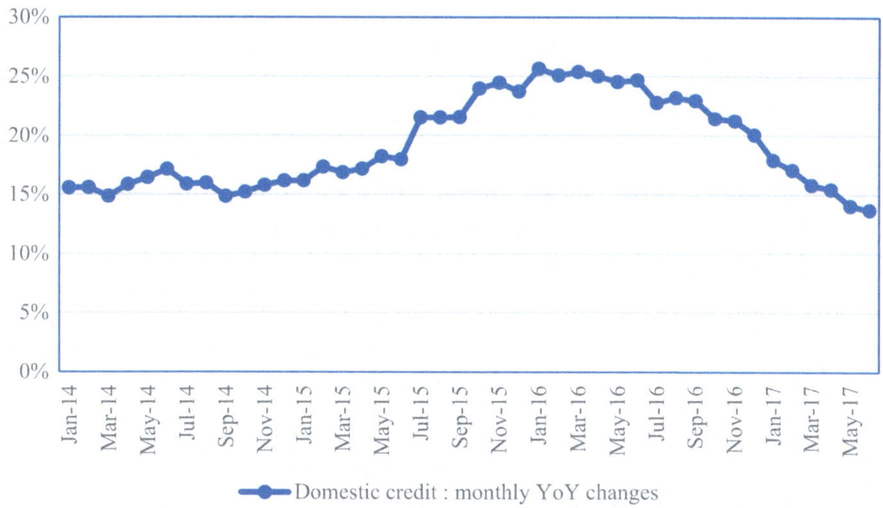

Fig. 1.22 Growth of domestic credit continued to decline. *Source* CQMM team calculations on CEIC data

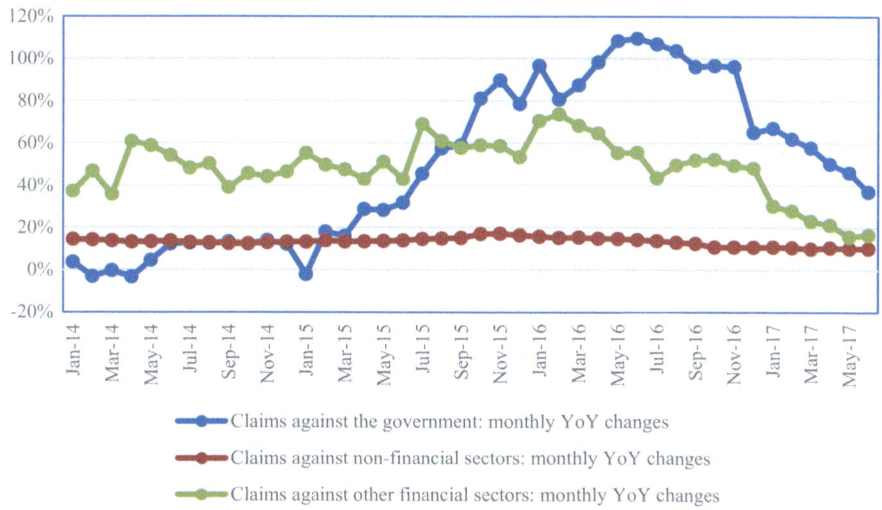

Fig. 1.23 The tightening of lending to non-banking financial institutions resulted in the decline in credit growth. *Source* CQMM team calculations on CEIC data

securities companies and trust companies; on the other hand, both the strengthened financial supervision and the regulation of local public finance affected the non-standard borrowing behaviors of various government departments significantly. These results met the target of China's financial deleveraging. Meanwhile, that lending to non-financial businesses did not tightened as a result of strengthened financial supervision also met the requirements of giving financial support for the real economy.

1.9 Proceeds from Transferring State-Owned Land-Use Rights Increased Substantially, While the Fiscal Deficit Expanded Strongly

In the first half of 2017, thanks to the resilience of the Chinese economy and the strong property market, revenues in China's general public budget rose by 10.3%, up 2.9 pcs over the same period a year earlier, 3.4 pcs more than the GDP growth rate. Of the government-managed funds, proceeds from transferring state-owned land-use rights surged by 34% to 1.88 trillion Yuan, up 0.48 trillion Yuan over the same period last year (see Fig. 1.24).

Fiscal spending continues to expand rapidly. In the first half of 2017, expenditures in the general public budget rose by 16.1%, up 0.7 pcs over the same period a year earlier. Of this total, expenditure items of the people's livelihood, such as social security and employment, health care and family planning, and education, all increased by more than 17%. In addition, fiscal spending on science and technology and urban and rural community affairs grew rapidly as well (see Fig. 1.25).

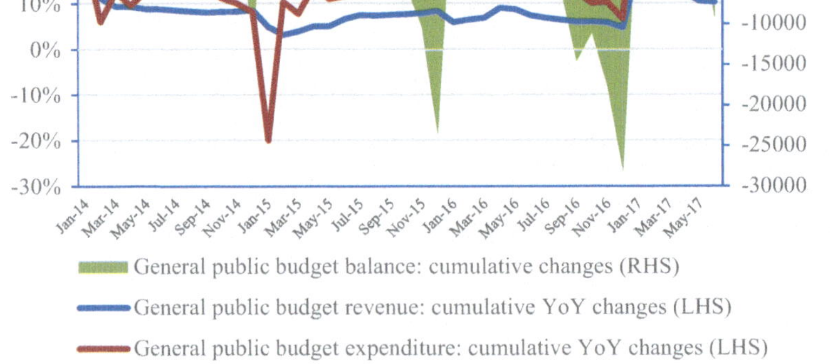

Fig. 1.24 Both revenues and expenditures in China's general public budget expanded significantly. *Source* CQMM team calculations on CEIC data

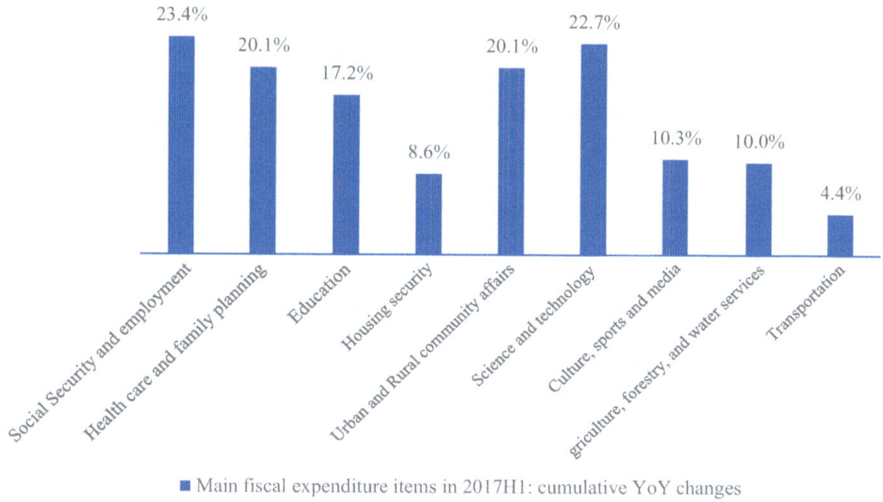

Fig. 1.25 Expenditure items of the people's livelihood grew markedly. *Source* CQMM team calculations on CEIC data

The fiscal deficit rose rapidly. In the first half of 2017, China's fiscal deficit reached 917.7 billion Yuan, an increase of 552.6 billion Yuan over the same period last year. The deficit ratio was 2.4%, still below the target threshold of 3%. The significant increase in the deficit mainly occurred in June 2017, when revenue in the general public budget reached 1.7082 trillion Yuan, up by 9.3%. Meanwhile, expenditures in the general public budget was as high as 2.71 trillion Yuan, up by 19.4%. In this one single month, the incremental deficit was up to 993.4 billion Yuan.

The sudden expansion of fiscal spending in the short term directly promoted the growth of infrastructure investment in June 2017, which turned from falling to rising, exceeding expectations. Causes of such expansion may be complex. One of them is that in the context of financial deleveraging and strengthened regulation on local public finance, the central government tried to avoid the risk of economic downturn by easing the fiscal policy.

In summary, the above analysis shows that, in the first half of 2017, the Chinese economy performed better-than-expected, driven by such factors as improved foreign trade, inventory replenishment, rapid expansion of infrastructure investment, strong property markets, and residential consumption resilience. Furthermore, with financial deleveraging and strengthened supervision of local public finance, the social financing still increased steadily, and financial support to the real economy was not affected.

Looking ahead, in the second half of 2017, the global economic recovery is expected to continue, and the growth of exports and shipping industry is set to be boosted; Meanwhile, the significant increase in value added of equipment industries in the first half of 2017 indicates that the upturn cycle driven by the equipment turnover and capital investment is on the way. And the escalation of rural consumption signs that the resilience of consumption is projected to continue.

The main factors expected to drag down the Chinese economy are: first, the cycle of inventory replenishment is projected to enter the downward phase in one quarter at most; second, although the growth of housing sales is still strong, from other indicators such as the growth of new housing construction area, the completion of the housing area, and land acquisition, the growth of real estate investment is set to edge down; third, infrastructure construction investment is largely constrained by the sources of government funds. Although there is still room to increase the fiscal deficit, the introduction of two documents, No. 57 and No. 87 by the Ministry of Finance, has blocked all the possible abnormal pathways from which the local governments are capable of borrowing money in recent years. As some of the infrastructure construction projects are unable to maintain due to lack of external financing, the investment in them is expected to face accelerating downward pressure.

In conclusion, with expanding foreign trade, stable investment growth, resilient consumption, improved financing structure set to provide solid support for the real economy, and driven by the political economy cycle such as the 19th CPC Congress to be held, the positive effects of China's economic supporting factors are expected to offset the negative effects of its dragging-down factors to a large extent. And thus, the Chinese economy is projected to remain relatively well in the second half of 2017.

Chapter 2
Quarterly Forecast for 2017–18

2.1 Assumptions on Exogenous Variables

2.1.1 GDP Growth of the United States and the Euro Area

In the first half of 2017, the global economy continued its good running posture since the second half of 2016. The US economy maintained fast growth after raising interest rates twice. The Euro area economy continued to recover and showed the best performance in the past ten years. Besides, the continued economic growth trend in Japan and emerging markets has been basically confirmed. The global economy has synchronized to a good trend for the first time since the outbreak of the international financial crisis. However, due to increasing protectionism in the world, the negative effects of the DPRK nuclear crisis on East Asia and the global economy, the frequent terrorism attacks occurring in Europe, much uncertainty of U.S. economic growth,[1] and so on, the steady growth of the global economy still faces many severe challenges.

In July 2017, the International Monetary Fund (IMF), while maintaining its April forecast of the global economy's growth rates for the next two years, revised substantially its growth forecasts for the US and the Euro area economies. Projected U.S. GDP growth rates were lowered to 2.1% in 2017 and 2.1% in 2018, down 0.2 and 0.4 percentage points compared with the April forecast, respectively. Projected Euro area GDP grow rate was rounded up to 1.9% in 2017 and 1.7% in 2018, up by 0.2 and 0.1 percentage points over the April forecast, respectively.

[1]The uncertainty of U.S. economic growth is reflected in: *a.* As in the early days of Medicare reform, the Trump government's tax reform and infrastructure plans are likely to fail through congressional approval, with the fetus dead; *b.* The Fed's moves to raise interest rates and shrink balance sheets have tended to be routine, with a shift in the global monetary policy environment that has persisted over the past few years.

China's Macroeconomic Outlook, Current Chinese Economic Report Series,
https://doi.org/10.1007/978-981-10-8096-8_2

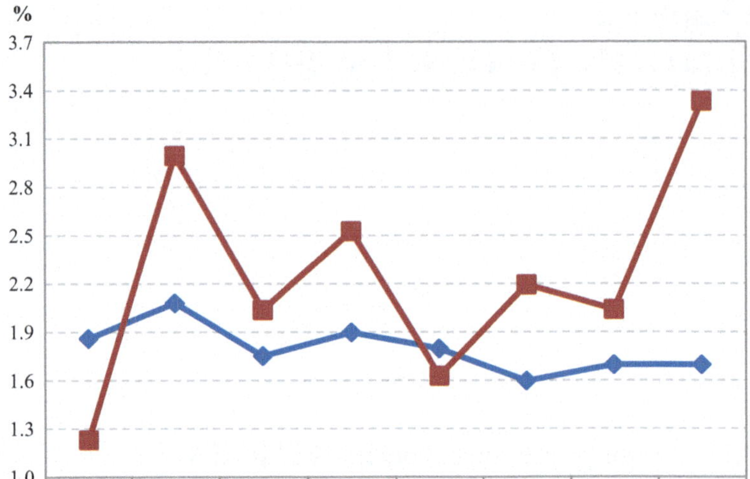

	2017Q1	2017Q2	2017Q3	2017Q4	2018Q1	2018Q2	2018Q3	2018Q4
EU_GDP_C	1.9	2.1	1.8	1.9	1.8	1.6	1.7	1.7
US_GDP_C	1.2	3.0	2.0	2.5	1.6	2.2	2.0	3.3

Fig. 2.1 Assumptions on GDP growth rates of the US and the euro, seasonally adjusted, QoQ. *Note* EAGDP_C denotes real GDP growth in the Euro area, USGDP_C denotes real GDP growth in the US. *Source* CQMM team assumptions

Based on the US economic performance in the second quarter,[2] the CQMM team assumes that the U.S. GDP would grow by 2.1% in 2017 and 2.2% in 2018, up by 0.1 percentage point over the IMF's July forecast. As to the Euro area, the team follows the IMF's July. Quarterly forecasts for the U.S. and the Euro area economic growth are shown in Fig. 2.1.

2.1.2 *The Exchange Rates*

The U.S. dollar index has fallen sharply after touching the top since this year. Though the Fed raised interest rates twice, the dollar did not stop depreciating substantially. Under this backdrop, various currencies, including the RMB, appreciate markedly against the dollar. At the end of May, China's central bank adjusted the RMB exchange rate mechanism with the introduction of counter-cycle adjustment factor, which changed the depreciation expectations of the RMB exchange rate. In addition, China's strong economic performance and rapid

[2]The U.S. economy saw a quick rebound in the second quarter. The QoQ annualized GDP grew to 2.6 from 1.2% in the first quarter. The Department of Commerce increased the second-quarter GDP growth rate to 3.0%.

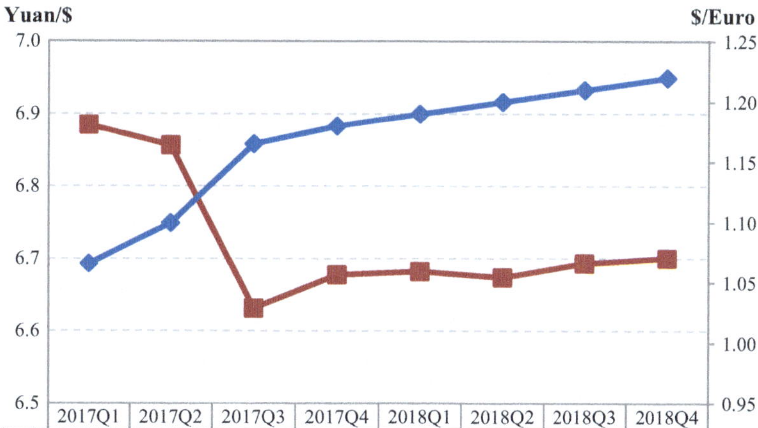

	2017Q1	2017Q2	2017Q3	2017Q4	2018Q1	2018Q2	2018Q3	2018Q4
ER_W	6.89	6.86	6.63	6.68	6.68	6.67	6.69	6.70
USDEURO	1.07	1.10	1.17	1.18	1.19	1.20	1.21	1.22

Fig. 2.2 Changes in exchange rates of the US dollar against the euro and the RMB to the US dollar, YoY. *Source* CQMM team assumptions

rebound in foreign trade growth in the first half of 2017 has not only largely supported the RMB appreciation, but effectively curbed capital outflows.

As the Fed is to shrink the balance sheet in October and likely raise interest rates at the end of the year, the dollar index is expected to rebound. Besides, given the above-mentioned outlook of the Euro area economy, the CQMM team assumes that the RMB exchange rate would stay stable with small volatility over the projection horizon. The exchange rate of RMB to US dollars is expected to be 6.68 at the end of 2017 and devaluate to 6.70 at the end of 2018 (see Fig. 2.2). On the other hand, the euro is projected to maintain appreciating against the dollar. The exchange rate of US dollars to euro is anticipated to be 1.18 at the end of 2017 and 1.22 at the end of 2018 (see Fig. 2.2).

2.1.3 The Broad Money Supply (M2)

The target growth rate of the broad money supply (M2) for 2017 was set at 12% in the work report by China's central government in March. In the first half of 2017, as the central government greatly strengthened financial supervision to counter systemic financial risk, the growth rate of M2 dropped to 9.51%. In the second half, taking into account the downward pressure of economic growth, the changing trend of inflation, and the change in the exchange rate of RMB to US dollars, the CQMM team assumed that China's monetary policy would keep a sound and tight tone over the projection horizon. The growth rate of M2 in 2017 is expected to remain at 10.5%, while in 2018 gradually fall to 9.5% (see Fig. 2.3).

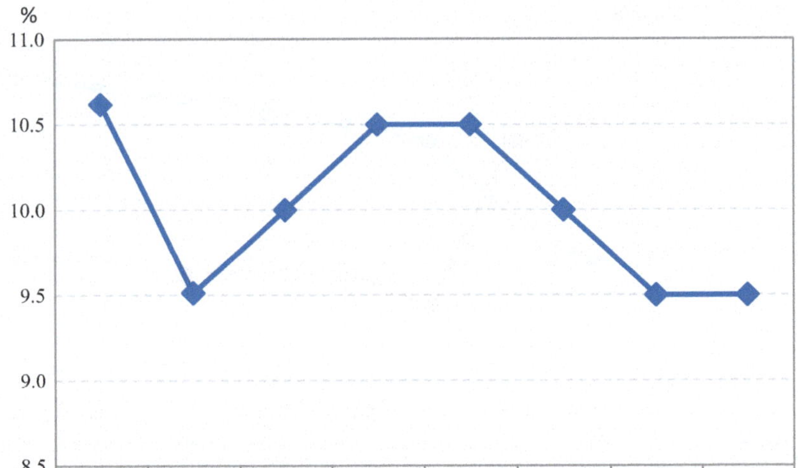

	2017Q1	2017Q2	2017Q3	2017Q4	2018Q1	2018Q2	2018Q3	2018Q4
M2_SA	10.6	9.5	10.0	10.5	10.5	10.0	9.5	9.5

Fig. 2.3 Assumptions on M2 growth (YoY). *Source* CQMM team assumptions

2.2 Quarterly Forecast of China's Key Macroeconomic Indicators in 2017–18

2.2.1 GDP Growth

Under the above assumptions on key exogenous variables in the China Quarterly Macroeconometric Model (CQMM), China's GDP is forecast to grow by 6.8% in 2017, up 0.1 percentage points over 2016. In 2018, China's economic growth is expected to edge down, declining to rise by 6.65%. Therefore, China's economy still stays in a gradually downward stage, and there is of little possibility occurring the so-called "China's New Business Cycle", which is characterized by a sharp rebound in economic growth.

Quarterly, in 2017, GDP growth is expected to fall to 6.74% in the third quarter and edge down to 6.66% in the fourth quarter, GDP growth in four quarters of the year showed a slow downward trend. In 2018, due to further improved external economic environments and domestic structure adjustment, GDP growth is projected to stay stable with small fluctuations. China's GDP is forecast to grow by 6.76, 6.73, 6.48, and 6.64% in the first, second, third, and fourth quarter, respectively (Fig. 2.4).

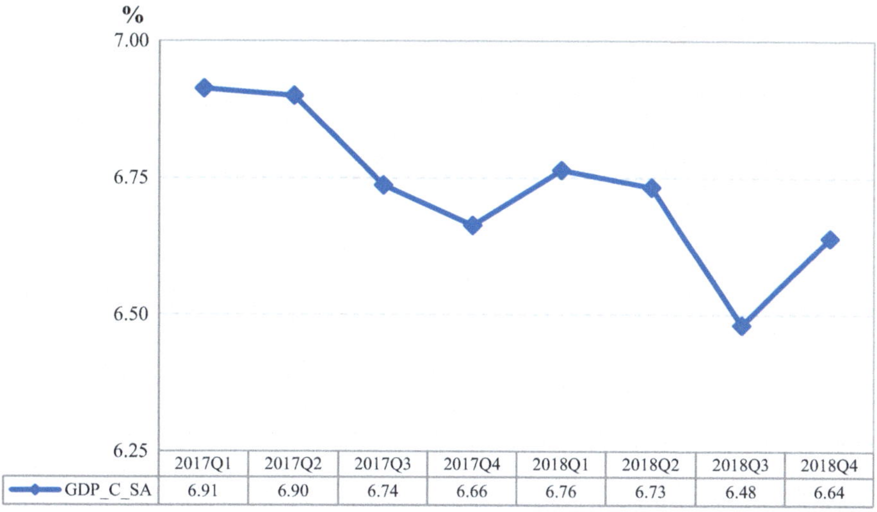

Fig. 2.4 Projected GDP growth rates (YoY). *Source* CQMM team calculations on CEIC data

2.2.2 Key Prices Indices

By the CQMM, the CPI is expected to rise by 1.72% in 2017, down 0.29 percentage points over 2016. In 2018, owing to increasing transmission effects of rising industrial prices, the CPI is projected to pick up to 2.84%.

Quarterly, in 2017, the inflation rates in the second half is expected to be significantly higher than the first half, with 1.83 and 2.24% in the third and fourth quarter, respectively. In 2018, thanks to the base effect, the tail factor, and the increasing producer price index (PPI), the CPI is forecast to rise to 2.82% in the quarter, 2.99% in the second quarter, and then fall back to 2.72% (see Fig. 2.5).

The PPI began to rebound in the first half of 2017. Over the projection horizons, as the supply-side structural reform continues to push forward, the PPI is expected to stay stable at high. The PPI is projected to grow by 6.24% in 2017, up by 7.59 percentage points over 2016. It is anticipated to fall back to 5.28% levels in 2018. It is noted that, while the rise in PPI growth would be beneficial for upstream industrial companies to increase profits, it would put cost pressures on downstream companies and consumers.

Quarterly, in 2017, the PPI is expected to further increase to 6.36% in the third quarter and fall to 5.37% in the fourth quarter. In 2018, due to the high base effect of the first quarter of 2017, the PPP is projected to drop to 3.56% in the first quarter, rebound to 5.88% in the second quarter, and then sustained steady growth (see Fig. 2.5).

Affected by a significant increase in PPI, the GDP deflator is forecast to rise to 4.77% in 2017 and further go up to 5.47% in 2018. Quarterly, in 2017, seasonally

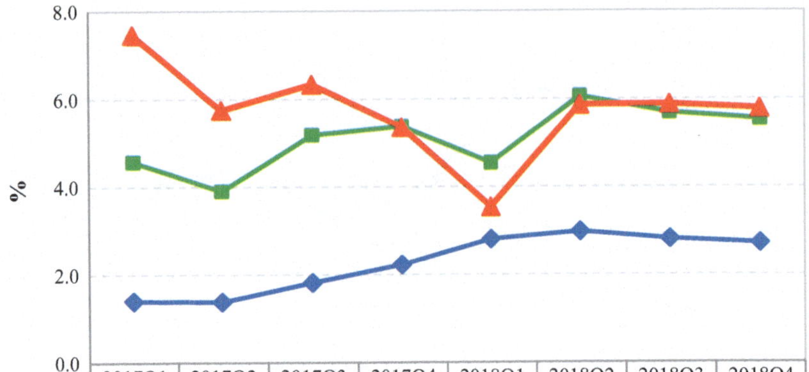

	2017Q1	2017Q2	2017Q3	2017Q4	2018Q1	2018Q2	2018Q3	2018Q4
CPI_SA	1.41	1.39	1.83	2.24	2.82	2.99	2.82	2.72
PGDP_SA	4.58	3.92	5.19	5.39	4.56	6.07	5.70	5.55
PPI_SA	7.49	5.77	6.36	5.37	3.56	5.88	5.89	5.79

Fig. 2.5 Projected growth rates of price indices (YoY, seasonal adjusted). *Note* PGDP_SA denotes seasonal-adjusted GDP deflators. *Source* CQMM team calculations on CEIC data

adjusted GDP deflator is anticipated to increase to 5.19% in the third quarter and further pick up to 5.39% in the fourth quarter (see Fig. 2.5).

In summary, over the projection horizons, the CQMM model predicts that China's inflation is expected to swell slightly, but still in a moderate controllable range.

2.3 Growth of Other Key Macroeconomic Indicators

2.3.1 Exports, Imports, and Foreign Exchange Reserves

Thanks to a synchronous recovery in the global economy, changes in China's export sectors and product structure, and effects by depreciation of the RMB exchange rate, China's imports and exports began to rebound in the first half of 2017. Over the projection horizon, the upward trend is expected to continue.

The CQMM model forecasts that, due to the base effect, the value of exports in dollar term (measured at current prices) is expected to grow by 7.9% in 2017, up by 14.37 percentage points over 2016, and in RMB term (measured at current prices) increase by 9.88%, 10.14 percentage points higher than 2016. The value of imports in dollar term (measured at current prices) is projected to rise by 16.18%, up by 21.79 percentage points over 2016, and in RMB term (measured at current prices) expand by 8.19%, 17.45 percentage points higher than 2016 (see Table 2.1).

Table 2.1 Projected foreign trade (%)

	Exports				Imports				Net exports as a share of GDP
	Current price/ RMB	Current price/US dollars	General trade at current price/ US dollars	Processing trade at current price/ US dollars	Current price/ RMB	Current price/US dollars	General trade at current price/ US dollars	Processing trade at current price/ US dollars	
2017	**9.88**	**7.90**	**6.37**	**7.94**	**18.19**	**16.18**	**22.25**	**10.16**	**1.31**
Q1	10.05	4.37	−0.26	9.19	30.57	23.83	31.12	13.36	1.26
Q2	11.65	6.36	3.88	7.35	19.83	14.15	17.50	11.60	1.21
Q3	9.09	9.67	9.62	7.16	14.96	15.57	21.41	8.22	1.24
Q4	8.76	11.25	12.52	8.12	9.66	12.18	20.19	7.77	1.51
2018	**6.16**	**7.37**	**9.50**	**6.55**	**9.60**	**10.84**	**15.43**	**5.61**	**2.52**
Q1	5.05	8.28	11.86	6.52	6.96	10.25	14.93	5.80	1.76
Q2	3.57	6.47	8.54	6.85	8.13	11.15	16.14	5.19	2.16
Q3	7.95	6.99	8.46	6.55	12.55	11.54	16.05	6.11	2.62
Q4	8.08	7.76	9.25	6.27	10.76	10.43	14.64	5.36	3.49

Source CQMM team calculations on CEIC data

Quarterly, in 2017, the value of exports in dollar term (measured at current prices) is expected to grow by 9.67% in the third quarter and 11.25% in the fourth quarter. The value of imports in dollar term (measured at current prices) is projected to increase by 15.57% in the third quarter and 12.18% in the fourth quarter.

In 2018, the growth of value of exports in dollar term (measured at current prices) is forecast to fall to 7.37%, down by 0.57 percentage points over 2017. The growth of value of exports growth in RMB (measured at current prices) is anticipated to drop faster to 6.16%, 3.72 percentage points lower than 2017. The growth of value of imports in dollar term (measured at current prices) is expected to reverse to 10.86%, down by 5.34 percentage points over 2017. The growth of value of imports in RMB term (measured at current prices) is expected to plunge faster to 9.6%, 8.59 percentage points lower than 2017.

The value of net exports as a share of GDP in 2017 is forecast to rise to 1.31%, up by 0.28 percentage points over 2016. It is anticipated to increase further to 2.52% in 2018. Affected by fluctuations in the exchange rate of RMB to U.S. dollars, and constrained by the new rules imposed by the central government on overseas investment, the pressure on China's capital outflow fell sharply in 2017. China's foreign-exchange reserves are expected to expand to 3.19 trillion dollars in 2017 and maintain almost the same level in 2018 (see Fig. 2.6).

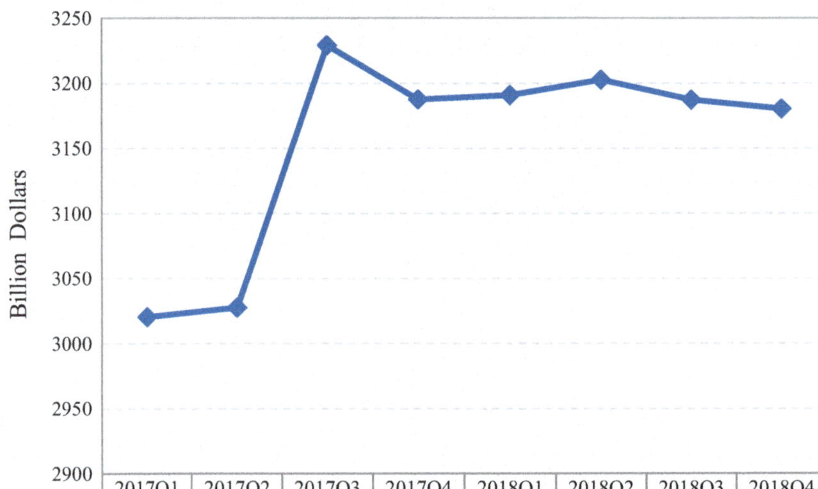

	2017Q1	2017Q2	2017Q3	2017Q4	2018Q1	2018Q2	2018Q3	2018Q4
FER_SA	3020.6	3027.7	3229.3	3187.8	3191.0	3202.8	3187.3	3180.5

Fig. 2.6 Projected changes in foreign reserves. Seasonally adjusted. *Note* FER denotes foreign exchange reserves. *Source* CQMM team calculations on data

2.3.2 *Growth of the FAI*

Based on the CQMM, the FAI (excluding farmers) measured at current prices is forecast to grow by 8.55%, up 0.21 percentage points over 2016; and slightly fall to 8.45% in 2018, indicating that the investment growth is expected to continue edging down.

Quarterly, the introduction of policies in the first half of 2017 to standardize local government financing behavior is anticipated to drag the growth of investment in the second half of 2017 by constraining the continuing expansion of government investment. The growth of investment is forecast to fall to 8.52% in the third quarter and 8.41% in the fourth quarter. In 2018, as the financial reorganization gradually reduced the risk of financial systemic risks, investment growth is expected to gradually stabilize. In the first quarter, with seasonal factors, investment growth is likely to rebound to 8.63%, but the next three quarters are expected to fall to 8.33, 8.44 and 8.41% (see Fig. 2.7).

In terms of sources of investment, the CQMM model forecasts that investment from domestic loans is expected to grow by 8.54% in 2017, a slight drop of 1.45 percentage points over 2016. In 2018 fall further to 4.4%. Due to continuous improvement of corporate profits growth in the first half of 2017, it is anticipated that the growth of investment from self-raising funds turn negative to positive in the third and fourth quarter, with 3.13 and 3.55% respectively.

Nevertheless, the investment growth of investment from self-raising funds in 2017 is projected to fall by 0.41%, making it one of the main cause for the decline

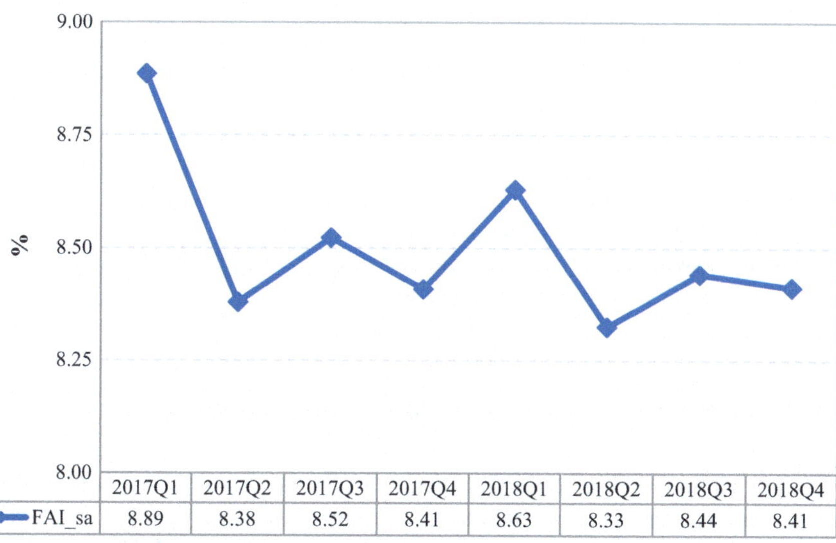

	2017Q1	2017Q2	2017Q3	2017Q4	2018Q1	2018Q2	2018Q3	2018Q4
FAI_sa	8.89	8.38	8.52	8.41	8.63	8.33	8.44	8.41

Fig. 2.7 Projected growth of FAI. Seasonally adjusted, YoY. *Note* FAI denotes the fixed assets investment. *Source* CQMM team calculations on CEIC data

Table 2.2 Projected growth of urban FAI by sources of funds (%)

	Total	Domestic loans	Self-raising funds	Others
2017	**2.95**	**8.54**	**−0.41**	**12.86**
Q1	−2.64	−1.64	−9.41	23.61
Q2	3.81	12.90	0.88	10.08
Q3	5.98	13.34	3.13	10.56
Q4	4.52	10.19	3.55	8.40
2018	**4.76**	**4.40**	**3.97**	**5.68**
Q1	5.81	8.73	5.54	2.72
Q2	3.55	0.54	2.87	3.24
Q3	5.15	3.95	4.25	8.65
Q4	4.62	4.74	3.41	8.22

Source CQMM team calculations on CEIC data

of annual investment growth. Owing to strengthened financial supervision, the growth of investment from other sources of funds is forecast to fall sharply to 12.86% in 2017, down 17.8 percentage points over 2016 and 5.68 percentage points over 2018 (see Table 2.2).

In conclusion, over the projection horizon, the investment growth is expected to maintain a steady downward trend. In the first half of 2017, although industrial production stayed stable and corporate profits rebounded, it is noted that the increase in corporate profits is closely related to the rebound in commodity prices. Besides, the increase in corporate profits is mostly concentrated in large state-owned enterprises, while the growth of private sector profits almost remained unchanged, which had greatly curbed the willingness of companies to make investment using self-raising funds. At the same time, the ongoing move of financial deleveraging and strengthening financial supervision restrained the expansion of off-balance-sheet operation by the financial institutions, which led to a sharp decline in the growth of domestic loan, and narrowed the funds and channels for enterprises to expand their investment. Furthermore, the introduction of a series of policies to standardize local government financing is anticipated to constrain the investment demand from local governments. Therefore, in the short run, the investment growth is expected to continue declining, and become the main factor to drag down China's rapid economic growth.

2.3.3 Growth of Residents' Income and Consumption

Although China's strong economic performance has ensured that the residents' income grow steadily, the continuous decline of labor productivity growth is dragging down the growth of residents' real income. The CQMM forecasts that urban residents' real disposable income per capita is expected to expand by 6.39%

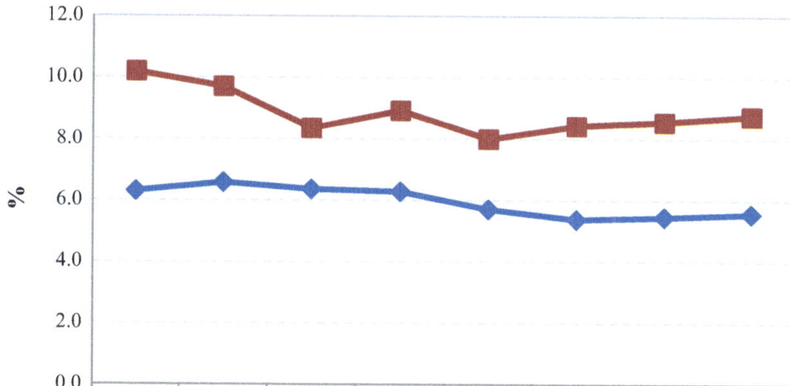

	2017Q1	2017Q2	2017Q3	2017Q4	2018Q1	2018Q2	2018Q3	2018Q4
Yd_u_c_pc	6.31	6.59	6.37	6.29	5.72	5.39	5.47	5.58
Yc_r_c_pc	10.20	9.71	8.36	8.94	8.00	8.43	8.57	8.77

Fig. 2.8 Projected urban and rural residents' income. *Note* YD_U_C_PC denotes urban residents' real disposable income per capita. YC_R_C_PC denotes rural residents' real cash income per capita. *Source* CQMM team calculations on CEIC data

in 2017, only 0.75 percentage points higher than 2016. It is projected to fall to 5.54% in 2018, down by 0.85 percentage points over 2017. Meanwhile, the rural residents' average cash income per capita is forecast to grow by 9.29%, down by 0.47 percentage points over 2016. And it is anticipated to further drop to 8.45% (see Fig. 2.8).

The continued expansion of residents' income growth ensured the steady growth of consumption. The CQMM forecasts that the total retail sales of consumer goods measured at current prices are expected to grow by 10.69% in 2017, a slight increase of 0.23 percentage points over 2016, and further increase to 11.83% in 2018.

Quarterly, the growth of the total retail sales of consumer goods measured at current prices is anticipated to rise to 11.24% in the fourth quarter of 2017, and further increase to 12.77% in the first quarter of 2018. In the rest of three quarters of 2018, it is forecast to edge down, but basically stay above the 11% level. Real household consumption is expected to grow by 6.67% in 2017, down by 1.57 percentage points over 2016. And slightly rise to 7.07% in 2018, up by 0.4 percentage points over 2017 (see Fig. 2.9).

In summary, the forecast based on the CQMM model indicates, over the projection horizon, the ongoing synchronous recovery of the global economy is expected to continue to boost China's foreign trade. Both the supply-side structural reform and the steady growth of domestic consumer demand is projected to tamp the foundation of China's economic growth. Nevertheless, due to high corporate and local government debts, strengthened financial supervision, and increased regulations on the property market, the rapid growth of investment is anticipated to

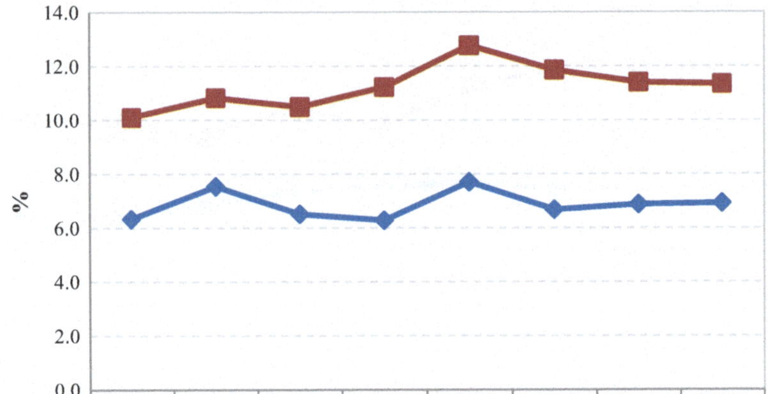

	2017Q1	2017Q2	2017Q3	2017Q4	2018Q1	2018Q2	2018Q3	2018Q4
CON_D_C_SA	6.34	7.54	6.52	6.29	7.71	6.69	6.88	6.92
RETAIL_SA	10.12	10.84	10.51	11.24	12.77	11.87	11.41	11.35

Fig. 2.9 Projected growth of consumption. *Note* CON_D_C_SA denotes seasonal adjusted growth rates of real household consumption (measured at current prices); RETAIL_SA denotes seasonal adjusted growth rate of total retail sales of consumer goods (measured at current prices). *Source* CQMM team calculations on CEIC data

be curbed. In summary, over the projection horizon, the Chinese economy is set to maintain a stable growth with continuous structural improvement.

1. Real GDP growth is expected to increase by 6.8% in 2017, 0.1 percentage points higher than that in 2016. The CPI is set to expand by 1.72%, 0.29 percentage points higher over 2016. The PPI is forecast to rise by 6.24%, up by 7.59 percentage points over 2016. The GDP deflator is anticipated to pick up by 4.77%, 3.65 percentage points higher than that of 2016.
2. The industrial production is expected to grow steadily, private investment is projected to rebound, and the fixed-asset investment (excluding farmers) is forecast to edge down. In 2017, the fixed-asset investment in current prices term is anticipated to grow by 8.55% in 2017, up by 0.21 percentage points over 2016.
3. The growth of real disposable income of urban and rural residents is expect to diverse, the income growth f urban residents is speeding up, while the income growth of rural residents is slowing down. According to current price, the total retail sales of consumer goods in 2017 are expected to grow by 10.69, 0.23% higher than 2016.
4. The strong performance of global economy is expected to continue boost China's exports over the projection horizon. In terms of current prices, the value of exports in U.S. dollars is expected to grow by 7.9% in 2017, up by 14.37 percentage points over 2016. The value of imports is projected to rise by 16.18%, markedly up by 21.79 percentage points over 2016.

Chapter 3
Policy Simulation: Effects of Changing Budget Constraints on the Non-financial SOEs

3.1 Background

China's central government has implemented various expansionary policies since the outbreak of the global financial crisis, which has led to a rapid rise in overall leverage in the economy. Both the massive implicit debt and the rapid growth of debt imply huge financial risks. Arising from excessive liquidity, financial speculation transmits and interact in different markets, areas, and sectors, which greatly increases systematic risks in China's economy.

3.1.1 The Significant Increase in Leverage Rate of the SOEs Is the Main Source of China's Financial Risks

Currently, the high leverage of non-financial enterprises is the main driver of China's high overall leverage rate. According to the debt-GDP ratio released by the Bank for International Settlement (BIS), the leverage of China's non-financial sector began to grow rapidly since 2008, increasing from 144.7% in the first quarter of 2008 to 257% in the fourth quarter in 2016. Of this total, the leverage of government sector expanded from 28.5 to 46.4%, the leverage of household sector went up from 18.8 to 44.4%, the leverage of non-financial enterprises leverage picked up from 97.4 to 166.3% (see Fig. 3.1). Non-financial firms have the highest leverage. By the end of 2016, the leverage of non-financial enterprises has exceeded the sum of that of government sector and household sector.

Among non-financial enterprises, the SOEs have the highest leverage, indicating that non-financial enterprises are the main source of China's financial risks. According to the BIS, the debt of SOEs accounted for about 75% of total non-financial enterprises' debt at the end of 2016. Meanwhile, the debt of non-financial

China's Macroeconomic Outlook, Current Chinese Economic Report Series,
https://doi.org/10.1007/978-981-10-8096-8_3

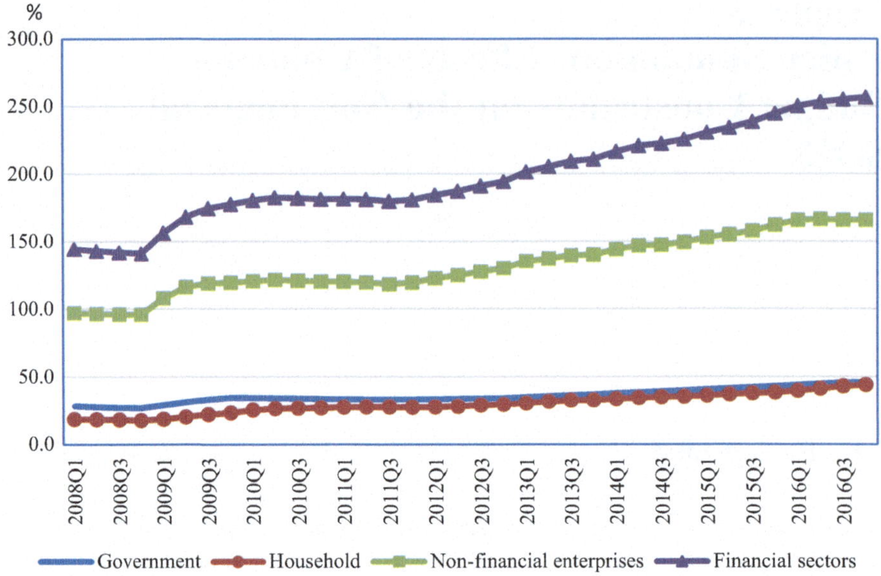

Fig. 3.1 Structural changes in the leverage of China's non-financial sectors. *Source* CQMM team calculations on BIS data

SOEs accounts for as much as 124.7% of GDP. If excluding the debt of non-financial SOEs, the debt ratio of non-financial non-SOEs is only 41.6%.

On the micro level, the change in the asset-liability ratio of enterprises also shows the same trend. Over the past decade, the asset-liability ratio of overall industrial enterprises has been declining steadily since 2008, falling from 59.2% in 2008 to 55.8% in 2016, while that of the SOEs rising from 61.6% in 2008 to 65.7% in 2016, up by 4.1 percentage points, and that of large-scale SOEs even exceeded 70%. In contrast, the change in the asset-liability ratio of private sector showed a downward trend, falling from 56.4% in 2008 to 50.7% in 2016 (see Fig. 3.2).

Therefore, the excessively high debt rate of China's non-financial enterprises mainly arises from the SOEs. The leverage of non-SOEs is not too high and is lowered gradually. This divergence does not only reflect the discrimination in the financial sector, but also undermines overall investment efficiency and leads to the accumulation of systemic financial risks.

Moreover, the solvency of China's non-financial SOEs is alarming. First, according to the BIS, the debt repayment rate[1] of China's private non-financial sector (including non-financial enterprises and the household sector) has picked up rapidly since 2008, climbing from 13.6% in the first quarter of 2008 to 20.1% in the fourth quarters of 2016.

[1]The debt repayment rate = Amount of principal and interest to be repaid at maturity/GDP.

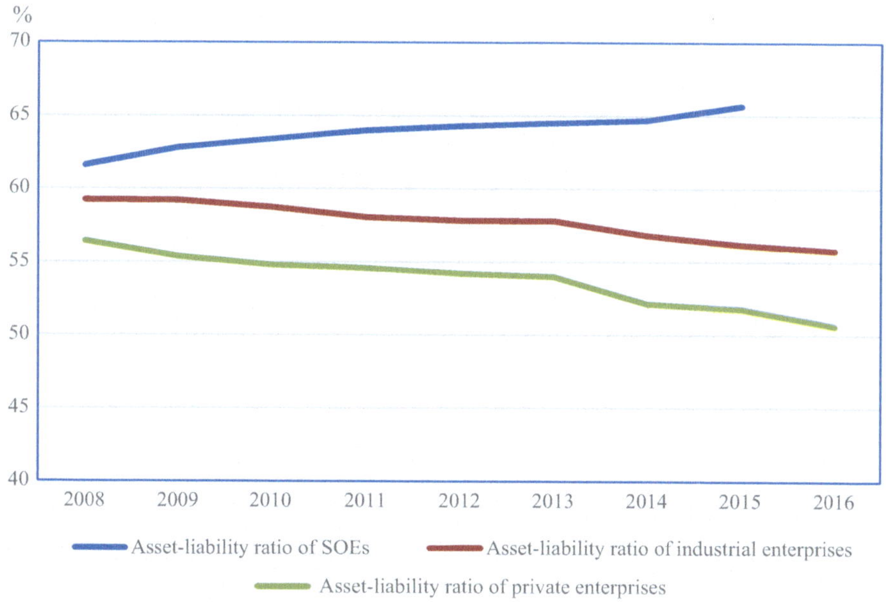

Fig. 3.2 Asset-liability ratio of the SOEs, private enterprises, and industrial enterprises. *Sources* CQMM team calculations on Wind Info & CEIC data

Second, since 2014, the interest reserve rate[2] of both industrial enterprises and private enterprises has declined significantly. Though interest reserve rates of industrial enterprises are still above 8%, that of the SOEs has fallen to a high-risk range of 2 in 2014.

Third, as to the turnover rate of enterprise capital, that of industrial enterprises gradually increased from twice in 2003 to 2.67 times in 2008, then fallen sharply to 2.43 times in 2009, then rose to 2.62 times in 2011, and then fell to the range between 2.5 and 2.6 times. Meanwhile, the liquidity turnover rate of the SOEs stayed at a relatively low level (see Fig. 3.3). Therefore, it is necessary to pay more attention to the solvency of the SOEs.

3.1.2 Main Causes of High Leverage of Non-financial SOEs

3.1.2.1 Excessive Macro Liquidity

Since the outbreak of the global financial crisis in 2008, China's central government has kept increasing money supply to boost economic growth (see Fig. 3.4).

[2]The interest reserve rate = Pre-tax profit/Interest charges.

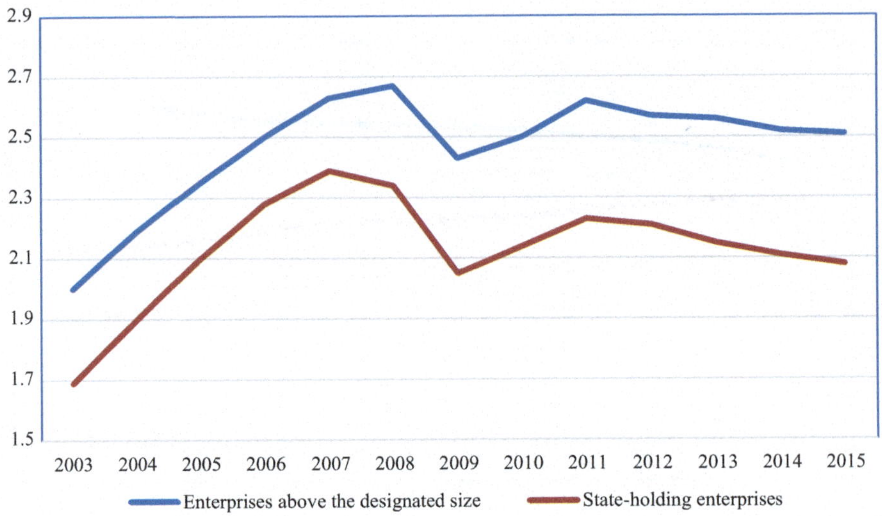

Fig. 3.3 Changes in liquidity turnover rate of industrial enterprises. *Source* National Bureau of Statistics

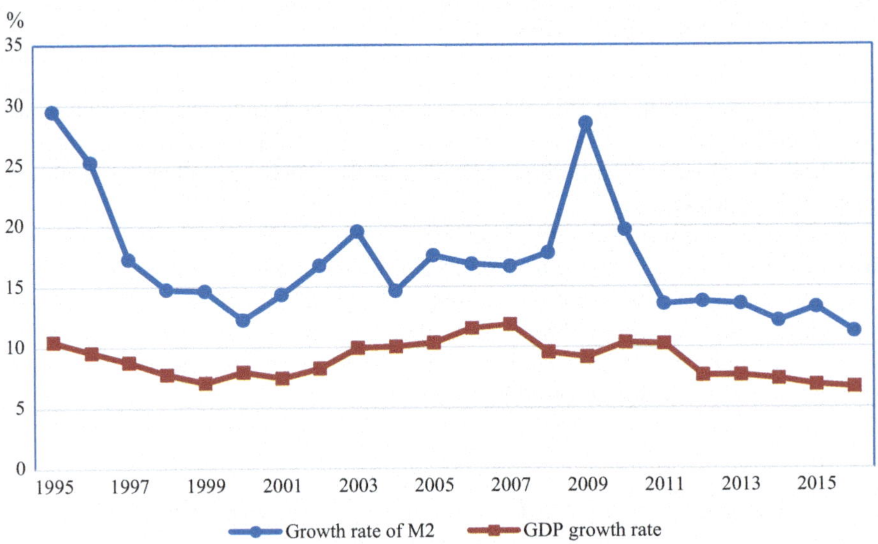

Fig. 3.4 Growth rates of M2 and GDP. *Source* China National Bureau of Statistics

Long-term excessive money supply has led to a steady rise in macro liquidity and a significant increase in the economy's monetization rate (M2/GDP), rising from 1.49 in 2008 to 1.74 in 2011, and further to 2.08 in 2016. The large amount of liquidity injecting into the economy, combined with the credit policy biased to the SOEs, provide good conditions for the high indebtedness of non-financial SOEs.

3.1.2.2 Financing Structure Dominated by Debt Financing

Due to underdeveloped direct financing markets, China's financing structure mainly depends on debt financing. And the relatively high bank indirect financing enhances the asset-liability ratio of the non-financial sector, especially that of non-financial enterprises. Moreover, national savings are mainly converted into bank deposits, which not only stimulates the expansion of the banking industry, but also gives the banks sufficient funds to provide credit support to the non-financial sector. As a result, it is quite convenient for the non-financial sector, especially non-financial SOEs, to increase leverage.

In terms of China's social financing structure, the share of debt financing, like bank loans, has been at a high level. In 2016, the share of debt financing in social financing reached 66.9%, while the share of domestic equity financing by non-financial enterprises was only 7% (see Table 3.1). Such a social financing structure dominated by debt financing increases enterprises' asset-liability ratio, and leads to high leverage. At the same time, as China's non-financial enterprises have high tax burden, in order to make full use of the tax shield effect, they prefer debt financing, which also promotes enterprises to increase the leverage.

3.1.2.3 The Development of Shadow Banking Has also Increased Markedly the Leverage of Non-financial Sectors, Especially Non-financial Enterprises

Moody's, the international rating agency, estimates that the size of China's shadow banking has risen from 19.2 trillion Yuan in 2011 to 64.5 trillion Yuan in 2016. And the size of shadow banking as a proportion of the total banking assets climbed from 18.3% in 2011 to 29.8% in 2016. Founder's Securities, one of China's securities company, estimates that the size of generalized shadow banking in 2010 was 15.5 trillion Yuan, 16.1% of the total banking assets, and 95.9 trillion Yuan in 2016, 41.6% of the total banking assets (see Fig. 3.5).

The reason is that financial innovation, deregulation, and monetary easing have increased the channels of shadow banking, stretched the chain of capital arbitrage, and pushed up the lever level among financial institutions, which led to the excessive expansion of shadow banking. In addition, high property prices brought about high returns on investment in real estate, encouraging social capital get away from the real economy and then get into the virtual economy, which also exacerbated the expansion of shadow banking.

Although under China's current financing structure, shadow banking may to some extent satisfy the financing needs of the real economy, due to implicit government endorsement, the easing money since 2014 has via the shadow banking system given financial support to the real estate, the local government financing platforms, and the state-owned zombie enterprises, which fully pushed up the leverage of the government and the SOEs.

Table 3.1 Social financing aggregates and its composition (%)

Year	Total (trillion Yuan)	Share of RMB loans	Share of foreign-currency denominate loans	Share of entrusted loans	Share of trust loans	Share of undiscounted bankers' acceptances	Share of corporate bonds	Share of financing via the stock market
2008	7.0	70.3	2.8	6.1	4.5	1.5	7.9	4.8
2009	13.9	69.0	6.7	4.9	3.1	3.3	8.9	2.4
2010	14.0	56.7	3.5	6.2	2.8	16.7	7.9	4.1
2011	12.8	58.2	4.5	10.1	1.6	8.0	10.6	3.4
2012	15.8	52.1	5.8	8.1	8.1	6.7	14.3	1.6
2013	17.3	51.4	3.4	14.7	10.6	4.5	10.5	1.3
2014	16.5	59.4	2.2	15.2	3.1	−0.8	14.7	2.6
2015	15.4	73.1	−4.2	10.3	0.3	−6.9	19.1	4.9
2016	17.8	69.9	−3.2	12.3	4.8	−11.0	16.9	7.0

Source The People's Bank of China

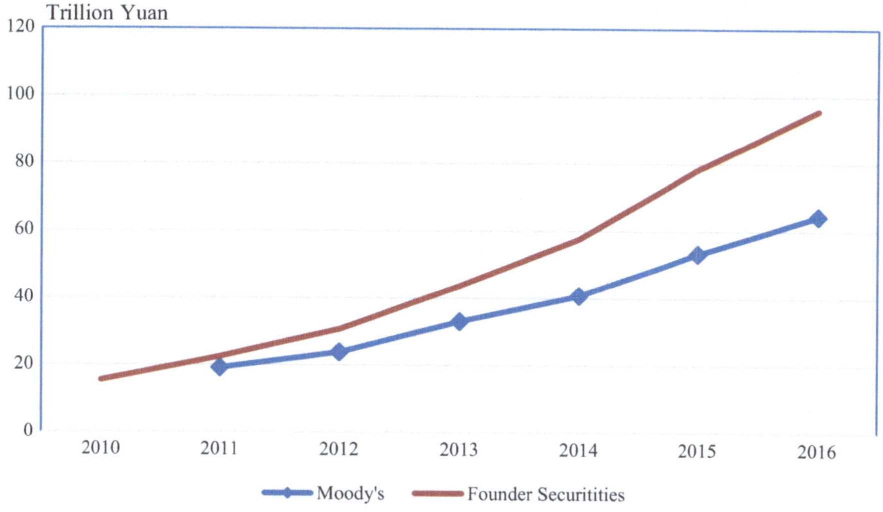

Fig. 3.5 Size of China's shadow banking. *Source* CQMM team calculations on CEIC data

3.1.2.4 The SOEs Face Soft Budget Constraint and the Loan Allocation Biased to the SOEs

For a long time, the allocation of bank credit resources has always been biased to the SOEs, while the private enterprises are difficult to obtain loans. Most of the money supplied by the central bank to boost economic growth over the past decade has turned into loans and then flowed to the SOEs. The excessive occupation of credit resources by the SOEs squeezes the financing of private enterprises.

Historically, China's state-owned banks bear the responsibility for financing the SOEs. As the loans to the SOEs often endorsed by the government, which lowers credit risks, the commercial banks preference to make loans to them. Furthermore, as the SOEs are mainly distributed in mining, chemical, construction, transportation, and other heavy industries, they themselves need more funds. The long-term existing soft constraint that the SOEs face motivate them to incur debt. Combined with the high cost of rigid payment and bankruptcy liquidation, the leverage of the SOEs is much higher than that of other enterprises. There even exists real estate enterprises which are too big to fail. Furthermore, the inefficient use of funds by the SOEs strengthens their demand for loans.

In summary, the SOEs have motivations to borrow money, while the banking industry is willing to make loans. As a result, the SOEs have significantly higher leverage than that of private enterprises. With the increase of the leverage of the SOEs, the dual-high leverage both of the financial sector and the SOEs has become the two major financial risk points of financial and non-financial sectors.

3.2 Simulation Plan

Based on the above analysis, the policy simulation of this report aims to explore the effects of putting hard budget constraint on the SOEs. The main idea of the policy simulation is: in order to control systemic financial risks from the source, we need firstly to tighten the money supply. Under the quantitative deleveraging policy of gradual tightening of money supply, the model designs two different scenarios: one is that the SOEs face soft budget constraint, the other is that the SOEs face hard budget constraint. And then we simulate and analyze the macroeconomic effects in these two scenarios, respectively.

3.2.1 Simulation Scenarios Planning

3.2.1.1 Counter-Factual Assumptions on M2 Growth

The simulation period was set from 2013 through 2015, covering 12 quarters. Over this period, the leverage of non-financial SOEs kept rising, making it a good realistic reference period for policy simulation. Over this simulation horizon, assume that China adopt a quantitative deleveraging policy that tightens the money supply. More specifically, assume that the M2 growth rate be lower than the actual values and the decline of it rising by 0.25 percentage points quarterly. As of the end period, the accumulated decline reaches 3 percentage points. The change in M2 growth and its balance over the simulation period are shown in Fig. 3.6.

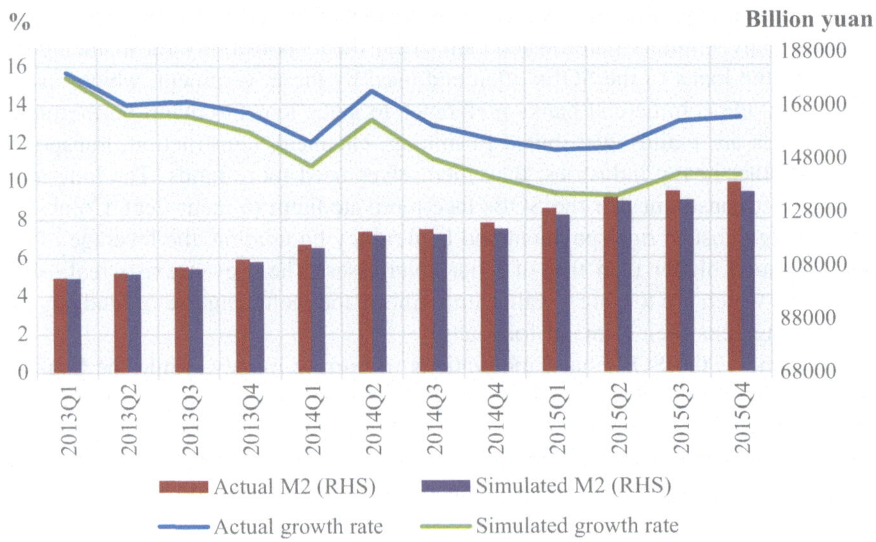

Fig. 3.6 Counter-factual assumptions and benchmark comparison of M2 growth from 2013 to 2015. *Source* CQMM team calculations on CEIC data

3.2.1.2 Counter-Factual Assumptions on Budget Constraints of Non-financial SOEs

Over the simulation period, assume that non-financial SOEs face two different budget constraints: one is the existing soft budget constraint, the other is the counter-factual hard budget constraint. Facing the soft budget constraint, the financing demand of the SOEs would always be satisfied, leading to increasing leverage. While facing the hard budget constrain, the financing demand of the SOEs would be affected by its leverage. When the leverage exceeds a certain threshold, the government would tighten the financing constraints on the SOEs, and the final actual financing amount is determined by the lower limit between the financing constraint and the financing demand.

3.2.2 Transmission Mechanism of Policy Simulation

As shown in Fig. 3.7, first, the SOEs' investment and private investment are determined by their own financing, among which the SOEs' financing has a competitive inhibition effect on the non-SOEs' financing. In other words, social financing always gives priority to state-owned enterprises, only the rest flows into non-SOEs. Second, the investment by the SOEs and non-SOEs does not only make up the total investment and determine the formation of capital, but also

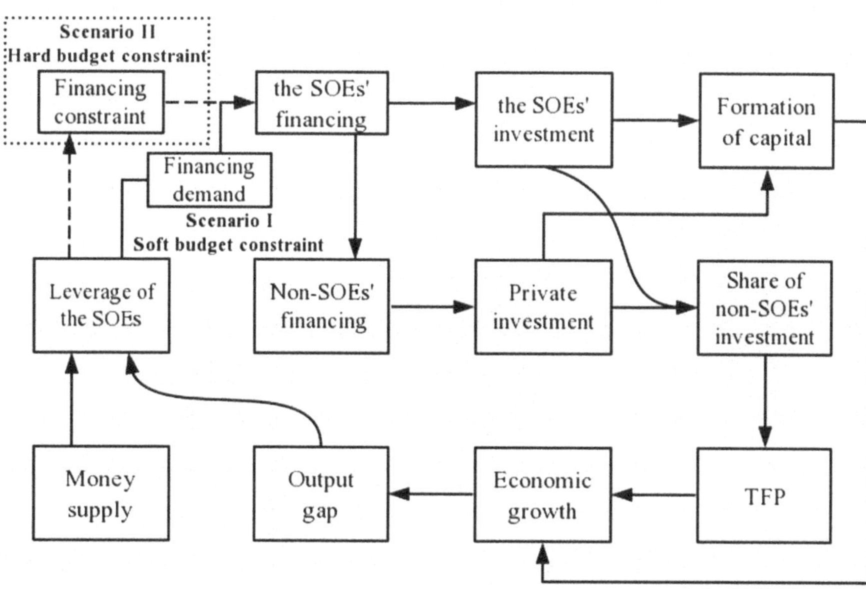

Fig. 3.7 Transmission mechanism of policy simulation. *Source* CQMM team

endogenously determines the share of non-SOEs' investment. Third, the share of non-SOEs' investment affects TFP, which further affects total output. Fourth, the deviation of total output from potential output affects local governments to boost investment and stabilize growth by increasing leverage on the SOEs.

3.3 Simulation Results

3.3.1 Scenario I *the SOEs Face Soft Budget Constraint*

In *Scenario I*, the SOEs face the soft budget constraint. The capital shortage caused by the reduction of the M2 growth would restrain the financing of the SOEs and Non-SOEs, and the growth of the SOEs' investment and private would both decline, which would negatively affect the growth of total investment in fixed assets (FAI). As shown by Fig. 3.8, over the simulation horizon, the growth of FAI is slower than that of the benchmark, and the decline continues to broaden.

Affected by the decline in investment growth, GDP growth decelerated against the benchmark value (see Fig. 3.9), which would stimulate the government to stabilize economic growth by increasing investment. As a result, once M2 growth slows, investment by the SOEs would decline due to the soft budget constraint. The decline of the SOEs' investment growth is relatively low, while the increase of their leverage is relatively high (see Fig. 3.10). On the other hand, as private investment

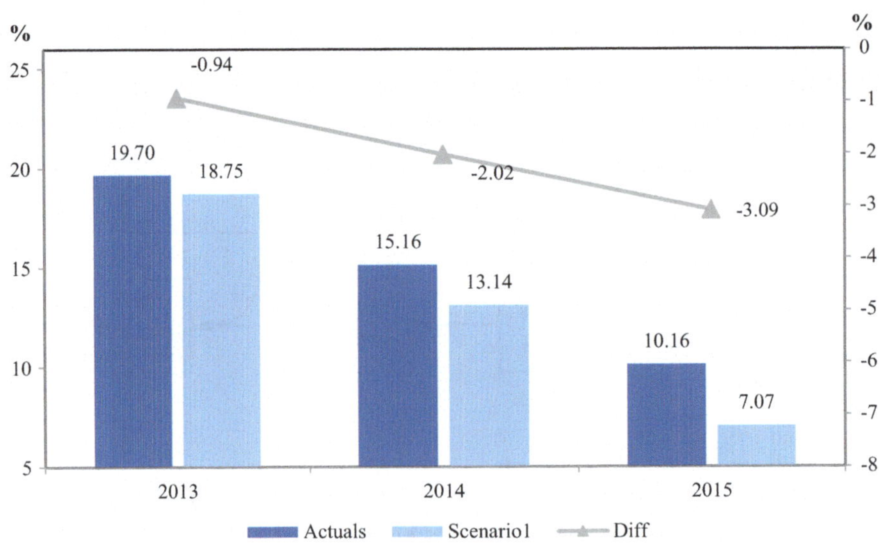

Fig. 3.8 Simulation of growth of total FAI. *Note Actuals* denotes the growth of investment when the M2 growth rate is the actual value over the simulation horizon; *Scenario 1* denotes the growth of investment after the M2 growth is lowered. DIFF denotes the difference between the simulated investment growth and the actual value. *Source* CQMM team calculations

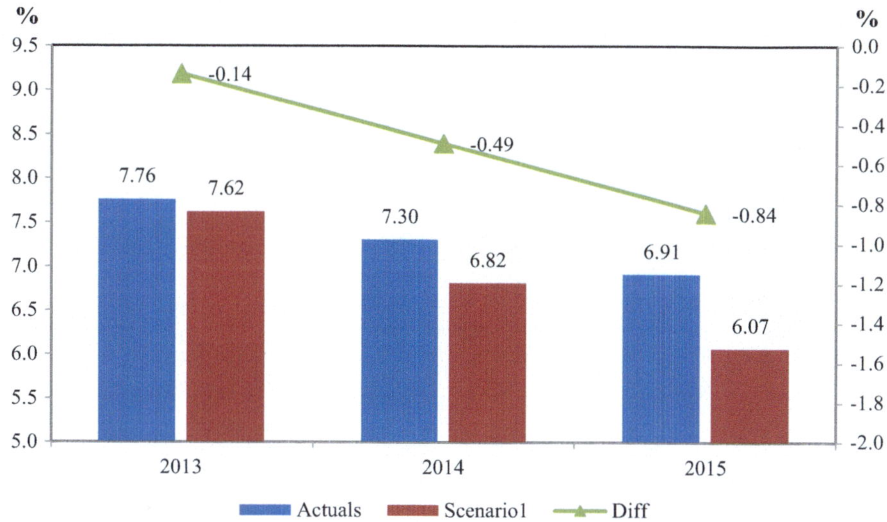

Fig. 3.9 Simulation on the change in GDP growth. *Note Actuals* denotes the growth of investment when the M2 growth rate is the actual value over the simulation horizon; *Scenario 1* denotes the growth of investment after the M2 growth is lowered. DIFF denotes the difference between the simulated investment growth and the actual value. *Source* CQMM team calculations

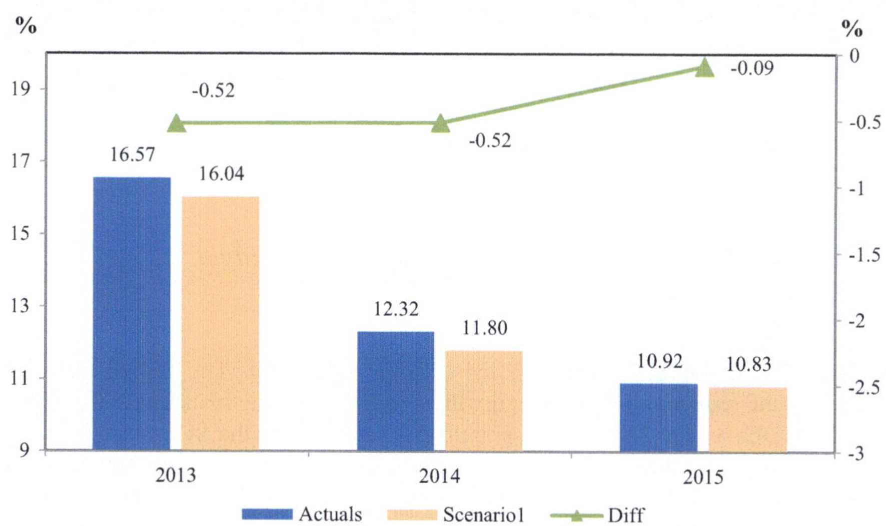

Fig. 3.10 Simulation on the growth of the SOEs' investment. *Note Actuals* denotes the growth of investment when the M2 growth rate is the actual value over the simulation horizon; *Scenario 1* denotes the growth of investment after the M2 growth is lowered. DIFF denotes the difference between the simulated investment growth and the actual value. *Source* CQMM team calculations

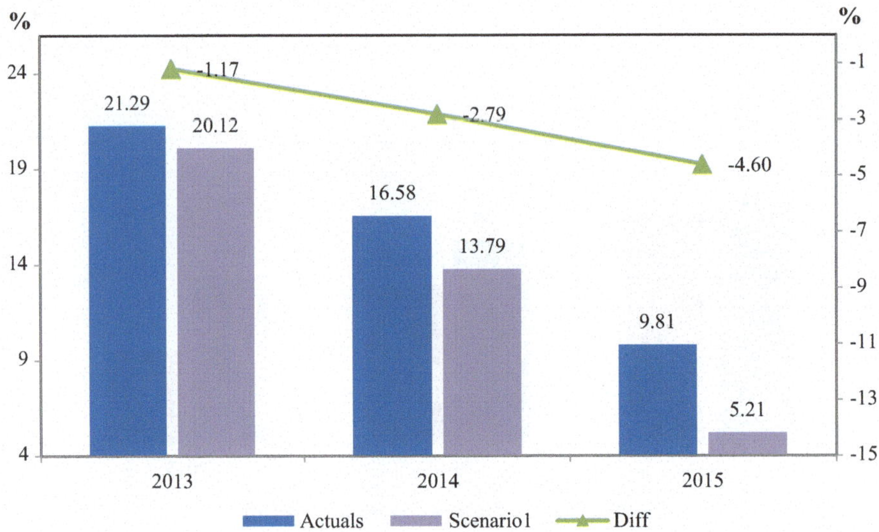

Fig. 3.11 Simulation on the growth of private investment. *Note Actuals*denotes the growth of investment when the M2 growth rate is the actual value over the simulation horizon; *Scenario 1* denotes the growth of investment after the M2 growth is lowered. DIFF denotes the difference between the simulated investment growth and the actual value. *Source* CQMM team calculations

would be squeezed by the SOEs, its growth would drop sharply (see Fig. 3.11). As the share of the SOEs' investment expands, their low investment efficiency would hinder the increase of TFP and have a negative impact on GDP growth. The expansion of output gap is likely to trigger a new round of boosting growth policy, leading to higher leverage of the SOEs.

3.3.2 Scenario II *the SOEs Face the Hard Budget Constraint*

In Scenario II, the SOEs face the hard budget constraint. The capital shortage caused by the reduction of the M2 growth would restrain the financing of the SOEs and non-SOEs as well. Nevertheless, unlike *Scenario II*, as the SOEs face the hard budget constraints, they could not continue to increase leverage to obtain investment funds. Furthermore, once the leverage of the SOEs exceeds a certain threshold, the credit line would be limited, and the financing constraint would be tightened. And thus, the growth of the SOEs' investment would not only lower than the actual benchmark value and that of *Scenario I*, but the decline of investment growth would broaden year by year (see Fig. 3.12). Meanwhile, although the growth of investment is lower than the actual benchmark value in each period, it would be higher than that in *Scenario I*. Besides, the decline in the growth

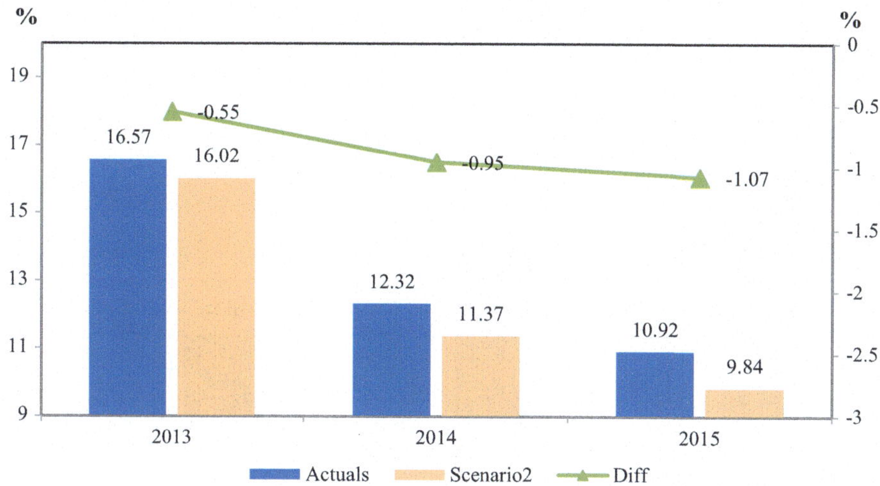

Fig. 3.12 Simulation on the growth of the SOEs' investment. *Note Actuals* denotes the growth of investment when the M2 growth rate is the actual value over the simulation horizon; *Scenario 2* denotes the growth of investment after the M2 growth is lowered. DIFF denotes the difference between the simulated investment growth and the actual value. *Source* CQMM team calculations

of investment would narrow significantly at the end of the simulation period (see Fig. 3.13).

In *Scenario II,* as the decline in the growth of private investment, which has a high proportion in total FAI, is relatively small, the decline in the growth of the FAI

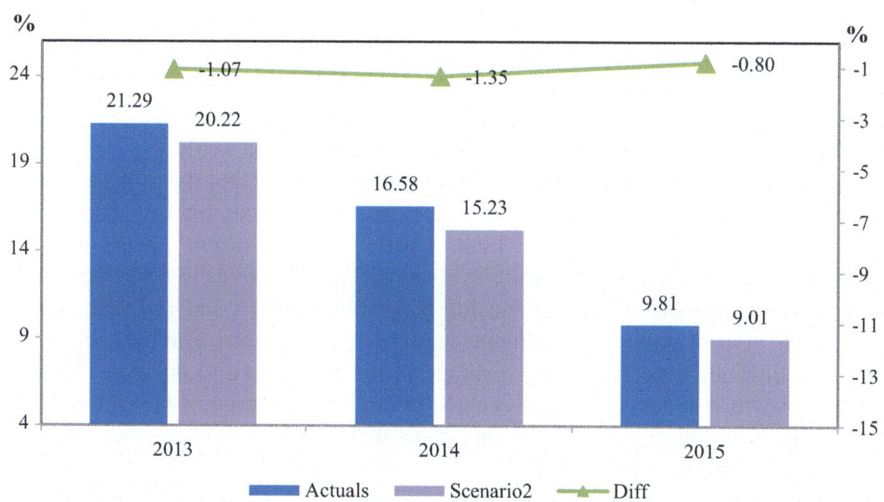

Fig. 3.13 Simulation on the growth of private investment. *Note Actuals* denotes the growth of investment when the M2 growth rate is the actual value over the simulation horizon; *Scenario 2* denotes the growth of investment after the M2 growth is lowered. DIFF denotes the difference between the simulated investment growth and the actual value. *Source* CQMM team calculations

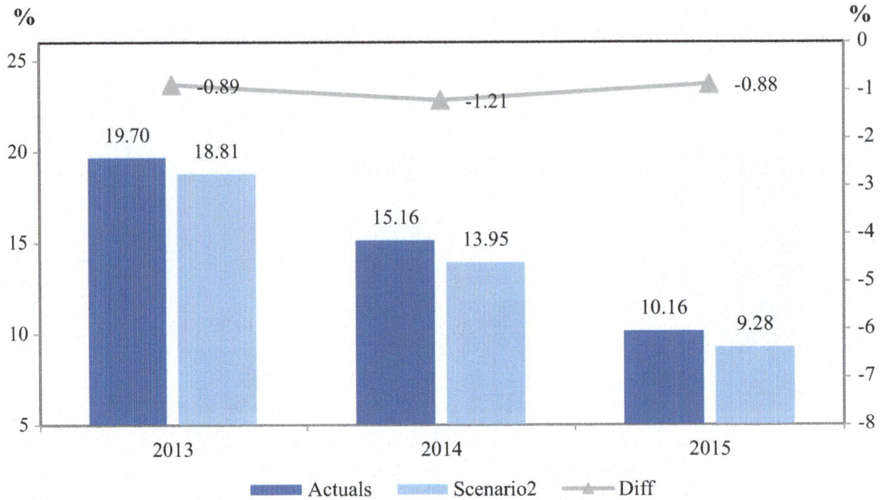

Fig. 3.14 Simulation on the growth of total FAI. *Note Actuals* denotes the growth of investment when the M2 growth rate is the actual value over the simulation horizon; *Scenario 2* denotes the growth of investment after the M2 growth is lowered. DIFF denotes the difference between the simulated investment growth and the actual value. *Source* CQMM team calculations

is also small (see Fig. 3.14). And thus, the effect of the decline in investment growth on GDP growth would be weakened. In addition, because the share of the SOEs' investment is hard to increase as such dramatically as in Scenario I, the effect of the reduction of M2 growth on the TFP is limited. As a result, at the end of each year over the simulation horizon, when the M2 growth declined by 1, 2 and 3 percentage points, respectively, the annual GDP growth decreased by 0.13, 0.31, and 0.27 percentage points, respectively (see Fig. 3.15). Furthermore, as the share of private investment increases, the efficiency of investment improves gradually, the TFP keeps rising, and the economic efficiency enhances markedly.

In summary, the simulation results show that, in the case that the SOEs face soft budget constraint, it cannot effectively reduce financial risks simply by reducing M2 growth and withdrawing money. First, under China's current government-led economic system, governments at all levels have strong motives to boost economic growth. As there exists close relationship between the SOEs and governments, to achieve the goal of policy, governments at all levels would strive to help the SOEs obtain credit line, which make the leverage of the SOEs hard to decrease. Even if the M2 growth is reduced by 3 percentage points, the leverage of the SOEs at the end of the simulation period is higher than the actual reference value by 0.25 percentage points (see Fig. 3.16).

Second, the fact that the SOEs face the soft budget constraint is in essence give them priority to obtain credits in the case of tight funds, which would shift most of

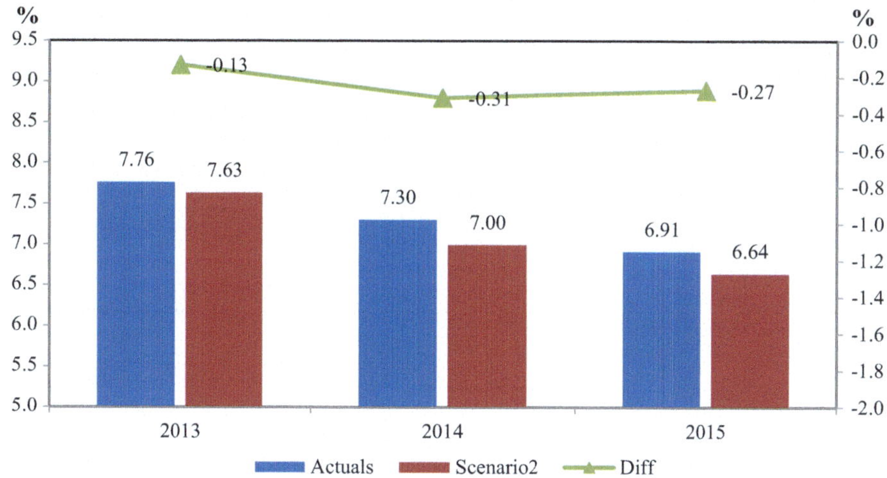

Fig. 3.15 Simulation on GDP growth. *Note Actuals* denotes the growth of investment when the M2 growth rate is the actual value over the simulation horizon; *Scenario 2* denotes the growth of investment after the M2 growth is lowered. DIFF denotes the difference between the simulated investment growth and the actual value. *Source* CQMM team calculations

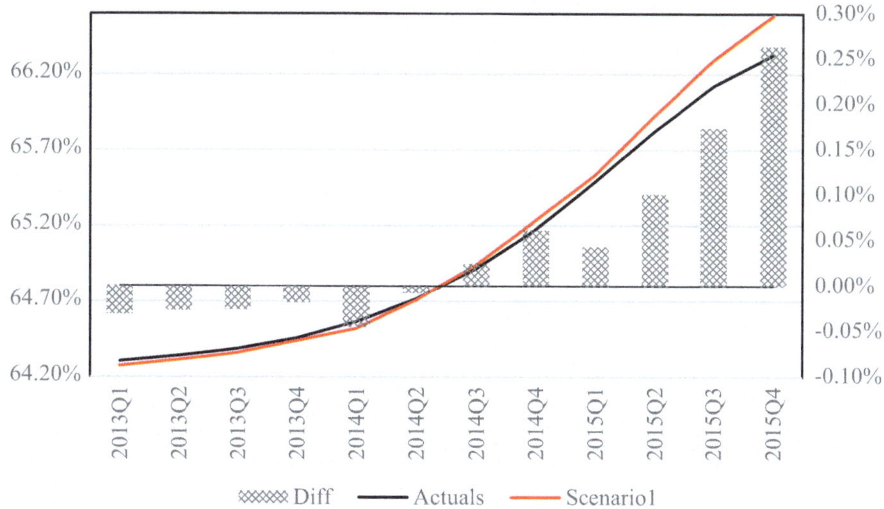

Fig. 3.16 Simulation on the change in the leverage of the SOEs. *Note Actuals* denotes the growth of investment when the M2 growth rate is the actual value over the simulation horizon; *Scenario 1* denotes the growth of investment after the M2 growth is lowered. DIFF denotes the difference between the simulated investment growth and the actual value. *Source* CQMM team calculations

the credit crunch pressure to non-SOEs. Such mechanism would not only have great impact on the growth of private investment growth, but also lead to the decline of overall social investment efficiency. As a result, economic growth would be dragged down significant, and the motive of thc local government to boost economic growth by increasing leverage would be strengthened further.

Chapter 4
Policy Implications and Suggestions

The above observations and policy simulations based on the CQMM model show that, to counter the potential systemic financial risks in China, we should not only eliminate the different risks in different markets, fields, and sectors, such as the high leverage of local governments, non-financial SOEs, and financial sectors, speculative chaos in real estate, the stock markets, the bond markets, and internet finance, shadow banking, and so on, but also eradicate root causes of systemic financial risks by deepening institutional reforms. We should ensure that the growth of money supply be almost parallel to economic growth, and endeavor to eliminate excessive money supply to strictly control the liquidity in the circulation. Moreover, we should establish China's modern public budget system and put hard budget constraints on the SOEs as soon as possible.

More specifically, the policy suggestions are presented as follows:

1. **The government should shift its focus on stimulating economic growth to provide more public goods and services**. China's current excessive liquidity and substantially increasing monetization rate (M2/GDP) stems from long-term excessive money supply. And the root cause of the long-term excessive money supply is the pursuit of high growth at all levels of government. After the global financial crisis, due to markedly reduced foreign demand, the growth of exports no more acted as a driver of China's economic growth. As the growth of consumption remained relatively stable, the task of the government to stimulate economic growth had to rely on expanding investment. Now that the non-SOEs reduced their willingness to make investment, governments at all levels had to enlarge their investment through SOEs. Due to the expansion of various government financing vehicles and the enthusiasm of SOEs to raise funds, the central bank had to increase the money supply. And thus, in order to stop the oversupply of money, we must relieve the pressure on governments at all levels. No longer take the GDP growth rate as heroes in the government performance appraisal. Instead, governments should gradually shift their focuses to the

China's Macroeconomic Outlook, Current Chinese Economic Report Series,
https://doi.org/10.1007/978-981-10-8096-8_4

provision of public services. As a result, let the government and the market function their own roles in the economy.

2. **Establish a rigorous modern government budget system and put hard budget constraints on the governments and the SOEs as soon as possible**. In order to avoid oversupply of money, the mechanism of hard budget constraints on the SOEs and the governments at all levels should be set up as well. In the short term, measures should be taken to put brakes on various behaviors of illegal and/or non-standard financing. In the long run, a standard and rigorous modern government budget system should be set up. Especially, with the establishment of a standardized local public debt issuance system, the problem that both governments and SOEs currently face soft budget constraints are expected to be solved.
3. **Take measures to withdraw excessively issued money gradually**. As non-financial SOEs are one of root causes of excessive money supply, in order to withdraw excessive money in the economy, we should introduce appropriate state-owned assets management system. Under the condition of fully safeguarding the state-owned assets, we can openly and fairly auction some SOEs in competitive areas. By steadily making the mixed ownership reform, promote the competitive field of state-owned monopoly industry to open to the private capital in time. Make the transition of state-owned assets management from physical management to asset management through the innovation of institutional mechanism. Furthermore, adjust the thinking of state-owned assets management to improve the operating efficiency of existing state-owned assets.
4. **Fully make use of various financial means to reduce the leverage of the non-SOEs**. China's current systemic financial risks is closely related to the long-term loose macro-liquidity management, and its root cause is that the priority of monetary policy is to satisfy the need for supporting GDP growth. In the long run, the aim of China's monetary policy should turn to serve more in keeping the currency stable and controlling inflation. To effectively control financial risks, China's monetary policy should strictly control the money supply, and coordinate with macro prudential supervision and financial stability policy. As the high ratio of debt financing is an important cause for the high leverage of non-financial enterprises, it is necessary to reduce the share of debt financing and develop equity financing to replace debt financing. In addition, reform the financial supervision system, and give full play to the function of capital market in reducing leverage and optimizing resource allocation. Strengthen supervision on commercial banks, prohibit non-banking financial institutions from making loans to the industry of overcapacity. Furthermore, actively carry out debt-to-equity swap to achieve the goal of deleveraging.
5. **Strengthen supervision on the shadow banking and let the financial system return to its intrinsic functions of allocating economic resources**. Combined with macro-prudential assessment System (MPA), strictly control the scale expansion of shadow banking, reduce the unregulated financing behavior, and actively guide shadow banks to give full play to the function of serving real economy. Over the past decade, the local government financing vehicles

(LGFVs) and the real estate kept adding leverage, and such sectors with lower efficiency as the SOEs and the LGFVs took up too much resources with implicit government endorsement and rigid payment, while such sectors with higher efficiency as private enterprises, manufacturing, and producer services were squeezed out. Therefore, we should continue to adjust the tax system, loosen the control over services sectors, strengthen the coordination of financial supervision, enhance returns on real economy, and make the idle capital return to the real economy.

Chapter 5
Appendix: Report on the Questionnaire Survey on China's Macroeconomic Situation and Policy in 2017

(September 2017, No. 9)

To keep abreast of the macroeconomic situation and policy trend, an annual questionnaire survey of China's macroeconomic situation and policy jointly started twice a year since the first time in August 2013, held by *the Economic Information Daily*, Xinhua News Agency and the Center for Macroeconomic Research, Xiamen University (one of the Key Research Institutes of Humanities and Social Sciences of the Ministry of Education of China). This is the ninth-time questionnaire survey about the study. There were 20 questions directly about China's macroeconomic situation and policy trend in the questionnaire, and we invited some domestic economists in relevant area for this survey by email in August 2017, and finally got responses from 121 of them. This survey offered the latest understandings and judgments of experts concerning the economic situation of the world, trends of some major indicators about China's macro-economy, and trends of China's macroeconomic policies in 2017.

The results of this survey are presented as follows:

1. **The global economy in 2017**

In accordance with the latest economic forecast of the IMF on July 23, 2017, the economic growth rate of the US would be 2.1% in 2017, and 0.2 percentage points lower than the forecast in April. Hence, we conducted a questionnaire survey on the trend of USA's economic growth in 2017. The survey reflected that 77% of the experts answered that the economic growth rate of USA would be "between 2.0 and 2.2%" in 2017. 15% claimed that it would be "between 2.3 and 2.5%". 7% claimed that it would be "1.9% or less". 1% of the experts thought that it would be "2.9% or more". Overall, nearly 80% of the experts believed that the US economy in 2017 would show a warming trend, and the situation is optimistic.

The IMF revised up the forecast for the economic growth rate of the Euro zone on July 23, to 1.9% in 2017 and 1.7% in 2018, compared with the forecast in April as 1.7 and 1.6%, respectively. We also conducted a questionnaire survey on the trend of Euro zone's economic growth. The survey reflected that 85% of the experts estimated the number would be "between 1.7 and 2.0%" in 2017.10% claimed that

China's Macroeconomic Outlook, Current Chinese Economic Report Series,
https://doi.org/10.1007/978-981-10-8096-8_5

it would be "between 1.3 and 1.6%". 3% claimed that it would be "between 2.1 and 2.4%". And 2% claimed that it would be "1.2% or less". In sum, more than 80% of the experts expressing a relatively optimistic expectation believed that the economy growth rate of Euro zone would show an upward trend and economy would be in recovery in 2017, the situation is optimistic.

In the first half of 2017, with the gradual recovery of the European economy, the Euro area began to get rid of deflation. And the euro rose to 1.1658 highest on July 20, which was higher than last year's highest point 1.1615. Hence, we conducted a questionnaire survey on the variation trend and range of the exchange rate of the dollar to the euro at the end of 2017. The survey reflected that 56% of the experts estimated that "the euro would continue to appreciate against the dollar, and at the end of 2017, the exchange rate of the dollar to the euro would be between 1.166 and 1.7", and the mean is about 1.2 (this question is gap filling). 37% of the experts claimed that it would keep stable. Another about 7% of the experts believed that the euro against the dollar would turn into depreciation, and the exchange rate of the dollar to the euro by the end of 2017 would be between 0.87 and 1.162, and the mean is about 1.093 (this question is gap filling). Overall, more than half of the experts believed that "the euro would continue to appreciate against the dollar", but the change would not be large, and there are about 40% of the experts claimed that "the exchange rate would remain stable" in 2017.

2. **The forecast of key indicators of China's economy in 2017**

According to the preliminary data released by China National Bureau of Statistics on July 18, growth rate of China's GDP in the first and second quarter are both 6.9%, so the growth rate of China's GDP in the first half of 2017 is 6.9%. How about the growth rate of China's GDP in 2017? The survey showed that 81% of the experts thought that it would be "between 6.7 and 6.9%", 14% expected that it would be "between 7.0 and 7.2%", and only 5% chose "between 6.4 and 6.6%". In sum, because the GDP increased by 6.7% in 2016, more than 90% of the experts considered China's economic growth would rise in 2017.

In the first half in 2017, China's CPI increased 1.4% compared to the same period of 2016, basically the same as the first quarter. The core CPI increased 2.1% excluding food and energy, and keep stable. How about the trend of China's CPI in 2017? The survey showed that 50% of the experts expected the growth rate of China's CPI would be "between 1.6 and 2.0%", 29% thought that it might be "between 1.1 and 1.5%", 21% held the view that it would be "between 2.1 and 2.5%". In sum, because the CPI increased by 2.0% in 2016, nearly 80% of the experts forecasted a certain downward trend of CPI in 2017.

In the first half in 2017, China's PPI increased 6.6% compared to the same period of 2016, and 0.8 percentage points lower than the first quarter in 2017. How about the trend of China's PPI in 2017? The survey showed that 50% of the experts expected that the growth rate of China's PPI would be "between 6.0 and 6.5%", 35% of the experts expected it would be "between 6.6 and 7.0%", 9% of the experts claimed that it would be "5.9% or less", and 6% of the experts believed that the growth rate of PPI in 2017 would be "between 7.1 and 7.5%". In sum, since the PPI decreased by 1.4% in 2016, so all the experts believed that the growth rate of China's PPI in 2017 would show a substantial rebound than 2016.

The exchange rate of the RMB to the dollar was 6.7415 by July 21 in 2017, which was the highest from October 20, 2016. About the exchange rate of the RMB to the dollar in 2017, 63% of the experts expected the RMB against the dollar would remain stable. 23% of the experts expected that the RMB against the dollar would continue to appreciate, and at the end of 2017, the exchange rate of the RMB to the dollar would be between 6.5 and 6.74 Yuan, and 6.61 Yuan on average (this question is gap filling). 14% of the experts believed that the RMB against the dollar would begin to depreciate, and at the end of 2017, the exchange rate of the RMB to the dollar would be between 6.75 and 6.9, and 6.8 Yuan on average (this question is gap filling). By December 28, 2016, the exchange rate of the RMB to the dollar was 6.9495. Therefore, all the experts believed that the exchange rate of the RMB to the dollar would be appreciate in 2017.

In the first half of 2017, China's investment in the fixed assets (excluding farmers' investments) was about 28.0605 trillion RMB, a nominal increase of 8.6%, 0.4 percentage points lower than the same period of 2016. How about the nominal growth rate of China's investment in the fixed assets in 2017? The survey showed that 51% of the experts expected the total fixed investments would increase year-on-year at the rate "between 8.1 and 8.5%", 43% considered that it would increase at the rate "between 8.6 and 9.0%", 4% chose "between 9.1 and 9.5%", 2% thought that the growth rate would be "8.0% or less". In sum, since the nominal growth rate of China's investment in the fixed assets in 2016 was 8.1%, more than 90% of the experts believed that the growth of China's fixed investments would begin to rise in 2017.

In the first half of 2017, the private investment in fixed assets was 17.0239 trillion RMB, a nominal increase of 7.2%. Private investment accounted for 60.7% of the total, and 0.3 percentage points lower than from January to May, 0.5 percentage points lower than 61.2% in 2016. Private investment growth continued to be lower than the national fixed asset investment growth, leading that the proportion of private investment for total investment continued decline. Thus, we investigated the reason (this question is multiple choice). The survey showed that 68% of the experts agreed that the new type of financing was difficult and expensive, and many policy-related factors led more credit to flow into state-owned enterprises or return to the financial system, which resulted in the crowding-out effect on private capital, together with the debt default problems of many private enterprises making financing more difficult and expensive. 65% of the experts claimed that private enterprises lacked confidence in the economy and the market outlook. 56% thought that the apparently strengthened financial regulation and deleverage policies affected the financing of small and medium private enterprises to some extent by raising the investment cost. 48% of the experts agreed that many industries such as the tertiary industry were still under control, with the investment areas being limited, the effective investment channels being narrow or pool, and the approval procedures for investment being cumbersome. 45% of the experts agreed that the lack of effective investment targets, the downturn of macro environment, plus the shrink and the falling profits of the traditional manufacturing industry, were leading to few effective and profitable investment targets for private capital. 36% claimed that the sustained upward trend of house prices squeezed the development space of the real economy and the private investment. Other reasons from the survey included the continued slowdown in the growth rate of the real estate investment after 2011.

Since last year, the growth rate of investment in fixed assets by source of funds has begun to stagnate, and even turned negative in the first half of 2017. From the perspective of its components, the main reason is the stagnation and contraction of the growth of self-financing funds from enterprises, together with the slowdown in the growth of other sources of funding and the stagnation of credit growth caused by financial deleverage. How about the growth trend of investment in fixed assets by source of funds in the second half of 2017? The survey showed that 66% of the experts expected a persistently negative growth rate mainly for the following several reasons. First, regulation and control on the real estate are difficult to relax, the situation of excess capacity in some industries are difficult to change, and the investment enthusiasm of enterprises is not high. Second, the outlook for enterprises earnings has not shown marked improvement, and the capacity of transforming the retained earnings into entity capital is limited. Third, the tight monetary policy and strengthened regulatory policy will maintain the current tone, and the space for external financing will be constrained. Forth, the economic outlook and policy expectations are unstable. Fifth, financial deleverage and sustained rise in production prices lead to increased financing and production costs and profits decline. Sixth, the causes of negative growth are hard to change in a short-term, etc. 29% of the experts expected the growth rate would turn to positive for the following reasons. First, economic growth rebounds, investment opportunities increase, and earnings relatively increase. Second, the economy grows faster than expected, and business confidence increases. Third, the 19th CPC National Congress will be held in the second half of 2017, and will create positive macro-environment expectations for the market system reform and the building of a good market environment, and the construction of traffic and other infrastructure will be further developed, etc. 5% of the experts expected the growth rate would be essentially stable, due to the reasons that the economic growth rate is in line with expectations, and there is an approximate balance between deleverage and steady growth, providing no reason for substantial expansion or tightening.

In the first half of 2017, China's investment in the real estate sector was about 5.061 trillion RMB, a nominal increase of 8.5% than 2016, and the growth rate was 0.3 percentage points lower than January to May in 2017. Among them, residential investment was 3.4318 trillion RMB, an increase of 10.2%. Residential investment accounted for 67.8% of the total investment in the real estate. How about the growth rate of China's investment in the real estate market in 2017? The survey showed that 65% of the experts expected it would be "8.1 and 8.5%", 18% expected that it would be "8.0% or less", 14% claimed that it would be "between 8.6 and 9.0%", 3% expected that it would be "more than 9.1%". In sum, compared to the first half in 2017, more than 80% of the experts believed that China's real estate market in 2017 would show a slowdown in investment, about 20% of the experts believed that China's real estate market investment would show a warming trend in 2017.

According to the first half year's national economic operation report released by the National Bureau of Statistics on July 17, 2017, five priority tasks were promoted solidly and policy results continued to show. In the first half of 2017, the national industrial capacity utilization rate was 76.4%, 3.4 percentage points over than the same period last year. So, How about the current situation in China's industrial sector? The survey showed that 39% of the experts agreed that "The speed of de production is moderate and in good condition", 27% of the experts agreed that "The speed of de production is slow, and affect the structure reform on supply side", 22% of the experts thought that "The speed of de production is a little fast, should be adjusted", and 12% of the experts thought that "The speed of de production is fast, should be based on the actual situation". In sum, nearly 40% of the expects thought that the speed of de production in industrial sector is moderate, and about 30% of the experts claimed to speed more, but other 30% claimed to slow.

In the first half of 2017, China's total social retail sales of consumer goods were about 17.2369 trillion RMB, a nominal increase of 10.4%. How about the growth rate of China's total retail sales of consumer goods in 2017? The survey showed that 72% of the experts expected the total retail sales of consumer goods would increase year on year at the rate "between 10.3 and 10.8%", 22% considered that it would increase at the rate "between 9.7 and 10.2%", 4% chose "between 10.9 and 11.4%", Each 1% of experts held the view that it would be "9.6% or less" and "more than 11.5%". So, the results reflected that compared to 2016, more than 70% of the experts maintained that the growth of the total retail sales of consumer goods would increase in 2017, and the role of consumption on economic growth would gradually be stimulating. However, nearly 30% of the experts thought it would show a decline trend in 2017.

In the first half of 2017, China's total exports was about 7.2097 trillion RMB, a nominal increase of 15%. How about the growth rate of China's total exports in 2017? The survey showed that 46% of the experts expected the total exports in dollar terms would increase "between 15.1 and 15.5%", 29% considered that it would increase "between 14.6 and 15.0%", 21% chose "14.5% or less", 4% held the view that it would be "between 15.6 and 16.0%". In sum, the results reflected that all the experts believed that the growth of the total exports would show a large degree of rise in 2017.

In the first half of 2017, China's total imports was about 5.9315 trillion RMB, a nominal increase of 25.7%. How about the growth rate of China's total imports in 2017? The survey showed that 31% of the experts expected the total imports in dollar terms would increase "between 25.1 and 25.5%", 27% considered that it would increase "between 25.6 and 26.0%", 21% chose "24.5% or less", 17% held the view that it would be "between 24.6 and 25.0%", and 4% chose "more than 26.1%" In sum, the results reflected that all of the experts believed that the growth of the total imports would show a large degree of rise in 2017.

3. **China's macroeconomic policy to be implemented**

By June in 2017, the balance of China's broad money supply (M2) was 163.13 trillion RMB, an increase of 9.4% than the same time in last year, 0.2 and 2.4 percentage points lower than last month and last year respectively. How about the growth rate of China's broad money supply (M2) in 2017? The survey showed that 63% of the experts had the expectation that it would grow "between 9.1 and 9.5%". 21% considered "between 9.6 and 10.0%". 14% chose "between 8.5 and 9.0%", 2% of experts maintained "between 10.1 and 10.5%". In sum, the results reflected that more than 80% of experts thought that the growth rate of M2 would be between 9.1 and 10.5% in 2017. It probably means the government of China would keep a moderate loose monetary policy in 2017.

According to the preliminary statistics of the People's Bank of China, in the first half of 2017, the scale of new Yuan loans was up to 7.97 trillion RMB in China, 436.2 billion RMB higher than the same period of 2016. Then, how will experts comment on where those new Yuan loans go (this question is multiple choice)? The survey showed that 75% of the experts believed that new Yuan loans didn't change the difficult and expensive situation of financing for private investment, 63% of the experts believed they ensured the expansion of investment in the field of infrastructure, 48% of the experts believed they didn't enter the real economy, leading to continuous drop in investment growth, 46% of the experts believed credit expansion was difficult to play effect due to poor monetary policy transmission channel, 30% believed they stimulated the expansion of the real estate market, and other 28% of the experts believed new Yuan loans accelerated investment growth for the state-owned and state-controlled enterprises.

The National Financial Work Conference which has been convened every five years since 1997 was held from July 14 to 15 2017, in Beijing. As Chinese President Xi Jinping pointed out, serving the real economy is the bounden duty and purpose of the financial sector, and the fundamental way to guard against financial risks. Therefore, we carried out a survey on the most anticipated three initiatives that would be considered to make financc serve for the real economy (this question is multiple choice). The survey showed that 69% of the experts chose the answer claiming that it is necessary to put the development of direct financing into an important position, and form a multi-level capital market system with perfect financing function, solid foundation system, effective market supervision and effective protection of investors' legitimate rights and interests; 56% of the experts chose "Improve the indirect financing structure, promote the strategic transformation of large state-owned banks, and develop small and medium-sized banks and private financial institutions"; 53% of the experts chose "Pay more attention to the stock reorganization, incremental optimization, and kinetic energy conversion of the supply side"; 50% of the experts chose "Construction of financial system, strengthen the financial services of small micro-enterprises, 'agriculture, rural areas and farmers' and remote areas, promote precision poverty alleviation by finance, and encourage the development of green finance"; 44% of the experts chose "Promote financial institutions to reduce operating costs, clean up the norms of intermediate business links to avoid disguised raise of financing cost for the real economy"; 15% of the experts chose "Promote the insurance industry to play a long-term sound risk management and security functions".

We also conducted a questionnaire survey on the room for implementation of China's fiscal policy in 2017 (this question is multiple choice). The survey showed that 73% of the experts chose "to clean up the funds and charges further, and then cancel, adjust, and regulate a number of administrative fees", 62% of the experts chose "to study and implement new tax reduction measures", 59% of the experts chose "to announce the directory list of central and local charges, and implement other tax reduction policies, which have been introduced", 56% of the experts chose "to continue to implement and improve the pilot reform of changing business tax to added-value tax, so as to expand the tax effect", 44% of the experts chose "to expand the scale of expenditure moderately, and the central and local finance should ensure immortalization of financial expenditure intensity and expansion of the actual expenditure scale through rational allocation of the budget and full revitalization of storage fund", 30% of the experts chose "to mainly use increased expenditures to cover expenditure requirements in priority areas".

In addition, we conducted a questionnaire survey on the major risks and response measures of our current economy (this question is blank filling). The survey showed that the experts believed the major risks of current economy in China are: (1) Real estate price bubble is serious, and there exists large financial risks; (2) Enterprises and local debt problems are serious, dragging up the level of bad debts in the banking sector, and will lead to systemic financial risks; (3) The economy lacks of new growth point, and we are unable to find measures to develop new industry; (4) Private investment lacks of sustainable growth rate; there exists uncertainty in international economic and financial environment, brought by Trump New Deal; (5) Economic downward pressure is difficult to ease; capital outflows. In response to the above risks, the main response measures include: (1) Strictly control the real estate prices, establish long-term mechanism of macro-control for China's real estate market price, so that real estate can return to normal residential function. Deepen the reform of the housing system, strengthen the top-level design of the real estate market regulation, speed up the establishment of a basic system and long-term mechanism which are in line with the national conditions and adapted to the market rules, maintain fair competition in the financial market and promote coordinated development of the real estate industry and the national economy. Meanwhile, implement the local government's main responsibility, and use various tools to suppress speculation. (2) Deleverage, and establish the relationship between the financial sector and enterprises to improve the business situation and reduce the debt risks; through political reform to limit the power of government at all levels, to limit government administrative expenses, to punish officials' corruption, and to adjust the income distribution; list local government balance sheet to make recessive debt explicit, and make local government debt service liability clear. (3) Increase self-innovation, to achieve self-improvement and self-deepening in traditional industries; try to activate the real economy, such as by real tax concessions, financing costs reduction by reducing financing links, implementing innovation drive for the real economic, etc. (4) Construction of PPP model for government departments and private capital to share the risks and profits, and promote the use of PPP model to attract more private capital to enter; speed up the market-oriented reform of investment areas, reduce the threshold of various types of market entry for private investment, especially to speed up the opening of water conservancy, railway and other monopoly areas, increase the opportunities for private capital and state-owned enterprises to compete and achieve win-win cooperation in the field of investment; guide private capital to enter more areas of innovation and development, to strengthen the classifying macro-control of the real estate market; create a better environment for development of private investment from the aspect of system construction such as financing environment, credit system and so on, increase tax cuts; strengthen the implementation and supervision of the policies regarding the encouragement of private investment, etc. (5) Promote the expansionary fiscal policy with the core of tax reduction to reduce the burden on enterprises and improve the investment environment, increase the disposable income of residents, and stabilize economic growth; promote economic reform and political reform, effectively ameliorate economic and political legal environment, and improve the expectation of investor and consumer for the future.

Table 5.1 outlines the difference between the CQMM team and experts forecast:

Table 5.1 Forecast of key indicators of China's economy by the CQMM team and the experts

Key indicators	By CQMM team (%)	By experts (%)	
		Interval	Ratio
GDP growth	6.80	6.7–6.9 7.0–7.2	81 14
CPI growth	1.72	1.6–2.0 1.1–1.5	50 29
PPI growth	6.24	6.0–6.5 6.6–7.0	50 35
Growth of total retail sales of consumer goods	10.69	10.3–10.8 9.7–10.2	72 22
Growth of total FAI	8.55	8.1–8.5 8.6–9.0	51 43

The manufacturer's authorised representative in the EU is Springer Nature Customer Service Centre GmbH, Europaplatz 3, 69115 Heidelberg, Germany. If you have any concerns regarding our products, please contact ProductSafety@springernature.com

Printed and bound by CPI Group (UK) Ltd, Croydon, CR0 4YY
25/09/2026
02222892-0014